we reconnected,
thanks to Facebook.
Good luck with
your book!
    Kay

A HEART TO SERVE

Twenty-Five Years in Haiti

Katherine J. Horning
and Martha J. Nordsieck

PublishAmerica
Baltimore

© 2012 by Katherine J. Horning and Martha J. Nordsieck.
All rights reserved. No part of this book may be reproduced, stored in a retrieval system or transmitted in any form or by any means without the prior written permission of the publishers, except by a reviewer who may quote brief passages in a review to be printed in a newspaper, magazine or journal.

First printing

Photography used in cover art provided by Andy Olsen.

PublishAmerica has allowed this work to remain exactly as the author intended, verbatim, without editorial input.

Hardcover 9781462651658
PUBLISHED BY PUBLISHAMERICA, LLLP
www.publishamerica.com
Baltimore

Printed in the United States of America

Bible verses in this book
are from
the New International Version
1978

Acknowledgments

The authors wish to thank Peg Weissbrod for her early editing contributions.

We are also grateful to Maureen Moore who obtained tributes from Magdala and Navius in Haiti.

Ms. Horning appreciates her husband's support and patience.

Both authors wish to thank Ms. Horning's daughter, Ellen Kemper, for her computer assistance.

Finally, we are indebted to Andy Olsen, both for his cover art and for his article in the Jan/Feb 2009 issue of Northwest Notes, as well as for his multimedia tribute, "Legacy of a 'Miss'" on the NWCHM website.

This book is about Pat Hamilton
who tirelessly served her Lord for
twenty-five years in two missions in Haiti.
She has been described by several people
as the most selfless servant of the
Lord they've ever met.

Although some of the book is fiction,
the authors have based it on actual events
in Pat's life in an effort to portray her strengths,
her spirituality, and her love and dedication
to the people of Haiti.

In creating new characters drawn from
a variety of individuals, the authors have
sought to communicate the essence of Pat's
experiences. As most of the dialogues are fictional,
names of Pat's family members and Haitian helpers
have been changed to reflect the authors'
imagination of events.

Likewise references to a
Midwest Christian College are
entirely fictional.

PROLOGUE

June, 1990

"Mis Pat, vini vit! Pressie! Nou gen yon pwoblèm! Anpil moun vini ak voodoo! (Come quick! Hurry! We're in trouble! The voodoo priest is coming! Many others too!)"

I had a blood pressure cuff on an elderly Haitian woman when I heard a frantic voice from the courtyard. I tore open the cuff and hurried down the hall to determine what the ruckus was all about. I could see my Haitian friend Liliane running toward me. As she got closer, she was visibly shaking and red in the face.

"What's going on?" I asked.

"Can't you hear the drums?" she gasped. "They've got a radio and are playing their horrible music. There's a whole procession dancing down the road waving banners and pounding their drums. They have many animals with them—chickens, goats, and pigs. I don't know what they're going to do, but they're headed to the big voodoo tree across the road."

The mission had just bought the land in front of the tree and planned to build a Christian church on that space. The voodoo priests had apparently heard of our plans and had come to try to stop us. What could we do? Most of the other missionaries were gone for the day.

"Gather your friends, Liliane! I'll get the folks here at the mission, and we'll block their way," I said, wondering if any Haitians would be brave enough to help us. I knew how frightened they were of the spirits that they believed lived in trees, especially Petro who they feared would mount them in the name of Satan. Those of us at the mission might be on our own in our effort to stop them.

I returned to the clinic where I hoped I could persuade my American friends Dave and Vicki as well as our Haitian doctor and nurses to come with me. I explained what was happening and asked for their help.

"We'll come," Dave said, but I could see fear and hesitation on Vicki's face.

"Not me," said Dr. Fadou, and I caught only a glimpse of the Haitian nurses all running out the back door of the clinic. It was clear how terribly afraid they were when I saw how quickly they vanished.

"Where's Jude? Maybe he'll come with us," I said.

But our Haitian medical assistant was nowhere to be found either.

"What's all the commotion?" I heard Donna's voice, as we left the clinic and started to cross the courtyard. We quickly filled her in on the situation.

"I'll help you, and I'll get Matt," she said, heading toward the pharmacy.

Soon there were six of us as we headed out the gate. By this time, the drums and music were really loud. I could see a sizable group coming up the lane. We hurried across, formed a line with hands joined, and began singing "A Mighty Fortress is Our God" in our strongest voices.

I'd never paid much attention to the words and their meaning before, but how appropriate they seemed this morning as we appealed to God to use his strength against this evil presence.

> "A mighty fortress is our God,
> a bulwark never failing;
> our helper He amid the flood
> of mortal ills prevailing…"

As we paused before the next line, Jude began reading from his Creole Bible in his loudest voice. He had come after all! I recognized the familiar words from Paul to the Ephesians.

> "Finally, be strong in the Lord and in His mighty power. Put on the full armor of God so that you can take your stand against the devil's schemes."

"Yes, God," I prayed aloud, "today we need your protection and mighty power as we face off against these believers in voodoo. Show us how to defeat their plans and safeguard this holy ground. In the name…"

Ouch, what was that? My eyes had been closed, but I felt a smack across my face. What had hit me? I looked behind me and jumped. A small black snake was coiled on the ground.

"I can't see," I heard Donna say in a shaky voice. "They threw some kind of nasty liquid in my face."

Bloody fluid was dripping across her cheeks and down her shirt. Matt, her husband, reached his arm around her protectively. She stood straighter with a determined look on her face.

"We can't let them get to the tree," she said. "That's where they want to worship their spirits."

"This is our land," I shouted in Creole "and God will help us build our church here in place of your tree!" As we tried to drown out their music with our own, we clasped hands and formed a human barricade.

> "…For still our ancient foe
> doth seek to work us woe;
> his craft and power are great,
> and armed with cruel hate,
> on earth is not his equal."

Surely God is bigger than the voodoo spirits, I thought.

Since we wouldn't let them cross our land, the angry group turned and walked around the perimeter to get to the tree. We hurried straight across and got there before they did.

"Look at the branches and leaves," Donna said. "See how they're bowing down to the ground and shaking."

"It's as if Satan has mounted the tree and is trying to scare us away," Jude added.

Sure enough, I could hear the branches cracking, and the leaves were falling all around us. I'd never seen a tree look so alive and frightening. However there was no wind to make it act like such a monster.

> "All the trees of the field will know that I the Lord
> bring down the tall tree and make the low tree grow
> tall. I dry up the green tree and make the dry tree
> flourish. I the Lord have spoken, and I will do it."

How had Jude known to look in Ezekiel to find such an appropriate scripture verse to read at that point? I wondered. What a brave Haitian Christian he was to stand up to these voodoo leaders and their anger.

The tree stopped shaking abruptly, and the voodoo contingent lowered their heads, turned around, and started back toward the hills, still beating their drums, but without the same confidence they'd shown earlier. As they faded from view, I heard a raucous *cocorico* from a rooster. It sounded like a wail of defeat.

We all looked at each other, fell to our knees, and offered thanks to God for protecting us.

"Lord," I prayed, "we thank you for your presence with us today and for giving us the courage to stand firm against these people who are your foes and ours. We ask that we will not have to face them again but will be able to build our church here on this ground that you've set aside for us. And Lord, please shine the light of your love in their hearts."

"Mighty God," Liliane continued in Creole, staring at the formidable tree. "I know that no Haitians will dare to cut down this stronghold of Satan. I pray that our American friends will be determined enough to get rid of it."

Our dear Christian sister had put into words a concern that revealed the powerful influence of voodoo, which permeates the culture.

As we crossed the lane, we closed and locked the gate behind us. Usually we kept it open during the day, but today we felt the need to be more secure after our frightening experience. Once inside the compound, I fixed us a pitcher of iced tea while Donna went to clean up and change clothes.

"I was so scared when they threw that stuff at us," Vicki said as we sat down around the table.

"Can you believe how that tree was acting? That was like something straight from a horror movie," Dave added with a shiver.

"Yeah, that really gave me the creeps," I said with goose bumps rising on my arms.

"Anyway we're safe now," Matt declared. "But I still wonder what we should do about the tree."

"A group of Americans is coming next month," I said. "They would cut it down. But what could we do with the wood?"

We all had different ideas about building something with it, but we realized that the Haitians would be afraid of occupying any room made with voodoo wood.

"I know," David exclaimed. "Let's use it to cook the food for the feeding programs."

"Great idea!" we all agreed.

When the rest of the missionaries returned that afternoon, we told them about the day's events.

"We really missed out on all the action, didn't we?" one man observed. "Praise God that he stood firm with you today."

CHAPTER ONE

September, 1983

"You want to do *what*?" my oldest daughter Susan said with disbelief. "Did you say that you want to move to Haiti to be a missionary?"

"You can't leave us. I'm only seventeen," Lynn, my youngest, cried out. "What would happen to me? Who would I live with?"

"Isn't Haiti a dangerous place, Mom?" asked my oldest son, Richard. "Are you sure that's a good idea?"

"You're fifty years old, Mom. I know you're strong, and Dad just died, so you might want a change, but why Haiti?" asked my stepdaughter Connie.

I had asked all my kids to come home for a Sunday dinner because I wanted to share what seemed to me to be a call from God. Ever since I'd heard Rosemary Austin speak at our little church in Southern Illinois two weeks previously, I'd been praying about whether helping her in Haiti was something God wanted me to do. I had anticipated that my family might question my thinking, but I hoped to persuade them that it was the right decision. Lynn certainly had a point since she was the youngest, and leaving her at the beginning of her senior year in high school did worry me.

"Hang on a minute," I heard my other son Steve saying quietly. "Let's give Mom a chance to explain. I'm not that enthused about her idea, but I'd like to hear more about her reasons."

Thank goodness I could count on Steve to hear me out. Many times since their father had been taken sick, his had been the voice of reason in the midst of family crises.

"Well, you see it's like this," I began, hoping that I could help them understand my aimlessness since my husband Bob had died a few months earlier. I had also lost my mother and my aunt and uncle during the previous year. It had been a very difficult time for me. I'd spent hours reading the Bible and asking God for guidance, and I needed a sense of purpose in my life.

"You and all our friends have been wonderfully supportive over this past year, but I've been feeling terribly restless and adrift. In Bible study a few weeks back, we were studying the passage in Matthew 25 where Jesus says, 'For I was hungry and you gave me something to eat, I was thirsty and you gave me something to drink, I was a stranger and you invited me in, I needed clothes and you clothed me, I was sick and you looked after me, I was in prison and you came to visit me…I tell you the truth, whatever you did for one of the least of these brothers of mine, you did for me.' "

I paused, taking a deep breath and exhaling before continuing. "Well, a thought came into my head, seemingly out of nowhere, and I told the people there, 'I'm going to be a missionary.' They were at a loss how to react, but it didn't matter to me. I had heard God's call. So when Rosemary spoke at our church a couple of weeks ago, it all seemed to fit."

"But Mom, can't you help people around here?" It was Lynn again. Obviously, she didn't want me to go so far away.

"I know, honey, it's you I'm most worried about. Your brothers and sisters are independent now with jobs and families and lives of their own. I've been thinking about how to make this time easier for you. I've wondered whether you could go live with Cheryl for senior year. What would the two of you think about that idea?"

I looked at both Lynn and Cheryl, her next older sister who was twenty-one and lived in an apartment nearby. I hoped to get a positive reaction, but I had sprung a lot on them and couldn't read their expressions.

"You mean I'd have to be her mother?" Cheryl blurted out. "I'd have to be responsible for seeing that she isn't out too late and be sure we'd have decent meals and get her to the doctor if she gets sick. I don't know that I'm ready for that job!"

"That's a lot of responsibility for someone who's still figuring out her own life's direction," Steve commented.

Were they right? Was I asking too much of my kids? I wondered.

"We don't have to make any major decisions tonight," I said. "Let's have some apple pie and play some cards before you all have to leave. Then you can go home and take some time to think, talk, and pray about what's best for everyone."

During the next weeks I continued to go to my nursing home job at Lutheran Care Center. One day Nora, my ninety-one year old friend who loved to tell me her family stories, asked me what was on my mind.

"You don't seem to be yourself lately," she said. "I've noticed that you don't stop to visit the way you used to."

How perceptive she is, I thought, as I wondered whether to share what was bothering me. I didn't want my manager, Miss Spence, to know that I might be leaving, but I did need someone to talk to.

"Can you keep a secret, Nora?" I asked as I shut the door to her room so that we could talk in private. Even though I wasn't supposed to spend a lot of time with one patient, I really needed to share my burden, and I trusted her to keep our conversation just between us. As we talked, I felt encouraged by the excitement in her eyes.

"Bless you, Pat," she said. "Not many women your age would want to take such a major step. If you feel that you're being called by God, then I think you should go."

What an affirmation to hear those words. Most people in their nineties would have thought I was crazy, especially since it would mean leaving Lynn during a vulnerable time in her life.

"You really think it's okay to go off and leave my family? I need to do something more meaningful with my life, and I know that I should probably wait another year or two, but this opportunity to help Rosemary with her Haitian clinic may not be available then. I've tried to push away the idea since I talked with my kids," I said, standing to go back to work, "but the urge keeps returning."

"I'd miss your caring presence," Nora said, "but others can fill in here, and not many would want to take the risk you're considering. You're talking about leaving all that's familiar for a radically different way of life. I'll pray for you to find clarity and peace about this. Now reach down here so I can give you a hug."

How reassuring and comforting it was to have her arms around me. Sensing a peace that I hadn't known in weeks, I took a deep breath and said, "Nora, thank you so much. I feel as if a huge burden has been lifted from my shoulders."

That evening, after Lynn finished her homework, we sat at the kitchen table eating ice cream and cookies. Fortunately, she's a smart girl and I wouldn't have to worry about her academically if I were gone.

"Tell me honestly, honey, how you feel about my leaving and your going to live with Cheryl. I need you to be frank with me."

"I'd miss you terribly, Mom," she said, swallowing to get rid of the lump in her throat. "It's been really special with just you and me here since Daddy died. I know how much you've missed him, but you've kept your chin up and we've become so close. It would be hard to have you so far away, especially in Haiti. I'd worry about you.

"On the other hand, I know how close you are to God. If he's calling you to minister in this way, as hard as it would be for me, you should go. I don't really like the idea, but I can see that you need a new direction in your life, and I don't want to stand in your way."

Her voice caught as she talked, and her eyes threatened to overflow.

"You've really touched me, Lynn. Your understanding means so much. Will you be okay with living with Cheryl?"

"Yeah, it's just until I graduate, and we get along fine."

Now I was the one with tears near the surface.

"Speaking of graduation, I'd try my best to be here, honey, but at this point, I just don't know if I could make it."

Lynn's face fell.

"Oh, Mom," she said, unable to hide her disappointment. "I really need you to be here for the ceremony. It will be hard enough not having Daddy there, but if you miss it too…" her voice trailed off.

"Well, it's still a long ways off, and I haven't even signed on with Rosemary yet, so let's not worry about it tonight. We'll cross that bridge when we come to it, and in the meantime, let's trust God to clear the way."

I was thankful Bob and I had been able to give all our kids, including our youngest, a solid foundation of self-confidence and faith. I gave her a quick hug as we both headed upstairs to bed.

CHAPTER TWO

About a week later my sister Enid called me one evening after dinner.

She had gone with me to the little church in St. Elmo on the night when Rosemary made her plea for someone to help her in the Haitian clinic for a year.

"So what have you been doing lately?" she asked.

"Nothing much. The usual—working, housework, you know how it is," I replied. "Why, what's on your mind?"

"Oh, I was just wondering if you were thinking of making any big changes in your life," she said. I could picture a smirky grin on her face.

"Are you a mind reader or something?" I asked. "I guess even though we didn't talk about it after Rosemary's speech, you could see that I was intrigued by her request."

"Yes, after fifty years of being your sister, I know you pretty well. So what's going on?"

I briefly touched on my conversations with Nora and the family and confided my concerns about leaving Lynn.

"But I can't seem to quit thinking about those children in Rosemary's pictures and how needy they are," I went on. "You know how much I love little kids. I think God really wants me to go for a year as Rosemary suggested."

"Well, how does your family feel about your going? Seems as if Lynn and Cheryl will be affected more than the others. What are they saying?"

"Based on a conversation with Lynn the other night, she's on board with it, but I haven't talked with Cheryl again. I suppose that would be the next step, wouldn't it?

"I also have to think about money," I continued. "In order to finance the trip and have something to live on, I'd probably need to sell the house. I haven't even mentioned that to the kids, and they might not like the idea."

"Yes, but the older ones already have homes of their own and Cheryl is in her first apartment. Think about it, how often do they come home?"

I had to admit she was right. Other than holidays or birthdays, we didn't get together very often. Richard was soon to be transferred to California with the Marines, Susan and her husband were married and living on the family farm, Karen was a full-time office assistant, and Steve had a good teaching job. They were all busy with their own lives. Even though Cheryl lived here in town, she was tied up with her banking job and social life and didn't get to visit very often.

"You're right, Enid. I'll look into listing the house with a realtor and see what happens. If it sells soon, I'll figure that's another sign from God. Thanks for calling. It's really helped to talk with you."

As soon as I hung up, I looked at the clock and decided it wasn't too late to call my realtor friend Velma.

"You're going where?" she responded incredulously. "When did all this come up?"

I explained what was going on in my life, and the next evening when I returned from work, there was a "For Sale" sign on the front lawn.

Suddenly it dawned on me that I hadn't told Lynn I was going to try to sell the house. Would this be an afternoon when she stayed late to work on the school newspaper? I certainly hoped so.

But as I pulled the car into the garage, the kitchen door opened, and there she stood with tears in her eyes.

"What's a 'For Sale' sign doing out front?" she demanded. "Why didn't you tell me? It's hard enough to lose you, but you never said anything about selling the house. How could you do this to me, Mom?"

She turned and ran up the stairs to her room. I started to follow but decided that she needed to calm down before we could talk. How on earth could I have goofed up so badly?

"Lord, help Lynn and me get past my thoughtless blunder. I'm afraid I've wrecked everything. Forgive me for my haste, and please heal our relationship."

When I unfolded my hands and looked up, Lynn was standing in the kitchen doorway.

"Mom, we need to talk. I was just beginning to be okay with the idea of your leaving for Haiti," she declared in an accusing voice, "but I didn't know that meant selling the house. You should have at least talked to us before you put it on the market!"

"Yes, you're right, Lynn. I had planned to talk with you tonight. I just called Velma last night on a whim, and I didn't realize she'd move so fast. All I can is I'm sorry, honey. Please forgive me."

I leaned on the table and put my head in my hands, regretting my impulsive call the night before.

"It probably won't sell right away," I said, raising my head. "It's fifty years old and needs some repairs."

"Maybe so, but it's been home to us kids for our entire lives. It's full of great memories of you and Daddy as we've all grown up."

What could I do to ease this uncomfortable situation? I wondered. Then an idea came to me.

"You know, I don't feel like cooking dinner. How about going out to eat for a change?" I asked. We very seldom ate out because I was on a tight budget, but it seemed like a good idea tonight. However, I wasn't sure that she'd want to be seen in public with me at that point.

She looked at me in amazement.

"I can't believe my ears!" she exclaimed. "We never go out to eat. Can we go to Sam's Place? That's where all the kids hang out."

I wasn't sure I could take all the loud music of a popular teen hangout, but if that's where she wanted to go, I'd agree to it.

By the time we returned home after dinner, raucous music, conversations with her friends, and several guys flirting with her, she was certainly in a much better mood. I couldn't say the same for myself, but I was glad that we'd gone.

Over the course of the next two weeks, Velma showed three potential buyers through the house. Each time she gave us little notice, so we always had to keep it picked up and ready for viewing. Again things moved very quickly, and in virtually no time at all, we had a contract.

CHAPTER THREE

One short month later I was on a plane from Miami to Port-au-Prince, Haiti. How quickly events had transpired during that month. As the plane taxied from the gate, I settled into my seat, thinking about how busy I'd been.

My kids had taken whatever furniture and other items they'd wanted, and we had moved Lynn's stuff into Cheryl's second bedroom. Then we'd held an auction to sell the rest of a lifetime's accumulation of things. I recalled my tearful goodbye with the residents of Lutheran Care Center, especially Nora.

"I'm sure I won't see you again in this life," she had said at my farewell party, "but rest assured you'll be in my prayers." I hadn't wanted Miss Spence to do anything special, but she had insisted on having punch and cookies for the residents and their families. I was humbled and moved by all the hugs and compliments I received that Sunday afternoon.

"Pat, we're going to miss your loving spirit," my manager had said. "You're so caring with the residents, and your sense of humor has defused some very volatile situations. I remember one time when Frieda and Henry nearly came to blows over the last cookie on the plate. After you told them a joke about sharing, neither one of them would take it! I'm sure that your love of God and humanity will touch many lives in Haiti," she'd added with a big hug.

I thought about the farewells with my family, especially the emotional good-byes with Lynn and Cheryl. My heart ached, so I reached into my backpack and took out my Bible. Before long, my eyes grew heavy and I must have dozed off.

"The pilot advises everyone to return to their seats for our descent into Port-au-Prince," I heard as I awakened.

Already? Have I slept through the entire trip? I must be exhausted, I thought as I looked out the window. During our descent, I could make out small shacks with tin roofs, dozens of people walking or riding donkeys or mopeds along the dirt roads, and brightly colored pickup trucks and vans traveling toward the airport. The wheels bumped on the runway, and we taxied toward the terminal. As soon as we touched down, the Haitians in the plane started gathering up their belongings in oversized plastic bags, eager to exit into the bright hot sun of the capital.

"Please remember your customs cards and have them ready when you enter the airport," the steward reminded us. Thank goodness I had taken care of that before I fell asleep. Someone from the clinic at Marchand Dessalines was supposed to meet me, but how would I recognize him? What if he didn't speak English? Now that I was actually in Haiti, I wondered about my decision and sent a quick prayer up to God.

"Lord, you've shown me the way so far. Calm my fears and give me courage. I'm putting myself in your hands. Amen."

I followed the other passengers down the stairs from the airplane and across the hot windy concrete pad toward the terminal. Even though it was October, the temperature felt like at least 90 degrees. I'm not in southern Illinois anymore, I thought.

I made it through customs with little difficulty. The heat inside the airport was oppressive, but at least the customs official spoke English. I looked around as I approached the baggage area, hoping to identify someone who might be waiting for me. Would I see a sign with my name? I wondered how anyone would find me in this sea of humanity until I noticed that I was one of only four or five white folks in the area.

I stood around nervously for a few minutes. Maybe I should go to the baggage carousel and retrieve my luggage. I had packed everything that I thought I would need into two heavy suitcases.

Mine were easy to spot, for almost everything that came around the carousel belonged to the Haitian passengers and was packed in cardboard suitcases or large garbage bags secured with duct tape. What should I do now? I wondered. I needed to find a restroom but was afraid to leave the waiting area since I might miss my driver. I was thirsty, but I had been cautioned not to drink the water in the airport.

I sat down in a chair surrounded by a host of black people with whom I couldn't communicate. How I wished I could at least carry on a simple conversation, but for now, a friendly smile would have to suffice.

"Are you Pat Hamilton?" I heard a pleasant voice say and looked up into a pair of warm brown eyes. A tall Haitian man stood above me with his hand outstretched.

I stood up and said, "Am I glad to see you!" as I shook his hand. "Yes, I'm Pat, and what is your name?"

"I'm Maurice, and I'm here to drive you to Marchand Dessalines," he replied. "I'm sorry I'm late, but I had trouble crossing the river outside Gonaïves since it rained last night."

"Isn't there a bridge?" I asked innocently.

"There used to be one, but it was washed out in last year's hurricane. Now we just drive through the water. It usually isn't much of a problem. Come this way."

"Before we leave, I need to use the restroom. Do you mind waiting?"

When I returned, Maurice picked up my luggage, and I followed him through the jostling crowd and out the door.

"Shall I get the jeep, or do you want to walk?"

"Let's walk. I need the exercise after sitting for two plane rides," I told him.

We wove through the waiting vehicles, some of which looked as if they wouldn't make it to their destinations. When we found Maurice's jeep, it looked no better, and I gave a silent prayer that God would help us get to where we were going.

Maurice drove out onto the street among many other cars and pickups, most of which were dented, missing headlights or bumpers, and some that were elaborately painted with Creole words.

"What do the slogans on those trucks mean?" I asked as we approached a particularly gaudy one.

"That one says 'Eternal God,' and the one over there says, 'Jesus saves,' " he replied, swerving to avoid a lady carrying several layers of eggs on her head.

He dodged in and out of traffic, blowing his horn as he went from one side of the road to the other. The noise from all the blaring horns was deafening.

Before long, we left the paved roads and began traveling over rutted gravel and dirt roads. Women balancing baskets or stainless steel basins filled with mangoes, papayas, clothing, and even sacks of charcoal atop their heads were walking alongside the road. An occasional child struggled with an unwieldy jug of water or a big plastic bottle of cooking oil. The men with their wheelbarrows or machetes were wearing shorts, but all the women wore dresses. I had to wipe my face frequently as sweat ran into my eyes. *How do these folks survive the long walks in this heat and choking dust?* I wondered, thinking that it was only ten in the morning. *How hot would it get later on in the day?*

Since the traffic and horn blowing had lessened as we traveled into the country, I struck up a conversation with Maurice. We talked about his job at the clinic, where he had learned English, and how long it would take to get to Marchand Dessalines.

"I learned my English from Miss Rosemary," he said. "I've helped her with whatever she needs for two years. Sometimes I put stitches in when someone has been cut by a machete. Other times I hold a child while she applies medicine and bandages up a bad sore or a burn from a cooking pot that has overturned. People come to us with all kinds of problems. Without Miss Rosemary, and now you, these people would have nowhere to turn for help."

I shook my head, wondering if I would be up to the challenges that lay before me. I certainly wouldn't mind holding a frightened child who was sick. That kind of service was my dream when I decided to come to Haiti. But machete cuts and burns? I shivered, despite the heat.

We bounced along in silence for a few minutes. Then, hoping to get started learning the language, I asked, "How do you say hello or good morning in Creole?"

"If it's morning, you say '*Bonjou*,' but at noon it changes to '*Bonswa*,'" he replied. "That means 'Good afternoon.' And if you want to ask someone's name, you can say, '*Kijan ou rele?*'"

Rounding a bend, he braked to a stop. "Well, here's the river. The water has gone down a lot since I crossed before," he said.

Carefully, he drove into the water that was lapping at a hole in the floorboard of the jeep. I picked up my feet to keep from getting wet. Maurice revved the engine and we bumped along the riverbed without any water coming in.

I looked out the side of the jeep at women doing their laundry, laying shirts and dresses on rocks and scraggily shrubs to dry, and bathing their naked children. Nearby, people were washing themselves. Two or three were even washing pickups and mopeds. I also noticed a young boy, clad only in a tee shirt, standing on the riverbank and peeing into the water.

"I see rivers have a lot of uses," I remarked.

"Yes, they are important to people's lives for many reasons. When it doesn't rain for a long time, it's a big problem."

About five hours into our trip, after going up yet another hill along the narrow rocky dirt road, the city of Gonaïves appeared below, spreading out from the ocean toward the surrounding foothills.

"When hurricanes come, water runs very fast down the hills and into the city because the mountains don't have many trees. People have cut them down to make charcoal so they can cook their food. The winds make huge waves in the ocean that wash into the city with great force. Many people die, trapped in their homes or swept away," he said, almost matter-of-factly.

I could scarcely imagine such horror.

We continued along the upper edge of the city and began heading inland into steeper terrain.

"These mountains are in the Artibonite region," Maurice informed me. "We'll soon be at the clinic if all goes well." I wondered what could go wrong.

We dodged emaciated Haitian dogs that scrounged for food in the middle of the road. People were riding or leading donkeys laden with bundles of sticks or woven saddlebags filled with bunches of bananas and other fruit. One man pulled a skinny cow up the hill. Her ribs were showing, and I wondered if she was actually able to give any milk. When a half dozen hens and roosters scattered out of our way, I marveled that drivers could miss all the people and livestock sharing these roads.

Half an hour later, we reached a small town where he pulled to a stop. "Well, here we are, hopefully in time for supper."

I looked around, relieved to see a small but substantial concrete-block house with windows and a corrugated metal roof.

"The clinic is in the front room, and you and Rosemary live in the back part of the house," he said, as I unfolded myself stiffly and stood up. "I'll take your suitcases to your room."

Well, God, here I am, I thought as I followed Maurice into the house.

CHAPTER FOUR

"Welcome, Pat, I'm so happy that you're here," Rosemary said with a big smile. "Our clinic gets terribly busy, and I sure can use your help. You are truly an answer to prayer."

"Did you have a good trip?"

I told her about my anxious moments at the airport, which seemed like an eternity ago. And how deeply the unrelenting poverty I'd witnessed had affected me, as well as the sheer foreignness of it all.

"Yes, that first impression is emotionally draining," she empathized.

"Come with me. I'll show you your room, and I'm sure you'd like to wash up."

I followed her into the front of the clinic.

"This room is where we see patients."

I looked around, noting how primitive everything was. I observed the concrete floor, the shelves that were sparsely filled and dusty, and the locked wooden cabinet.

"We keep our medicines and most equipment locked up so that our supplies don't get stolen," she explained. "People are desperate and some will steal to get money for food or rent."

Behind the clinic, Rosemary led me past a small kitchen.

"We'll come back here and have a Creole meal after you get settled," she said.

"Oh good," I said, wondering what my first Haitian meal would be like. "It's been a long time since breakfast."

"Here's your room, and mine is next to it. There's a bucket with soap and a washcloth on the stand in the corner, and the latrine is right out back."

I looked around at what would be my home for the next year. The room was probably 10x10 with a single bed, a dresser, and a small table and straight chair. There were two windows.

"You won't have to close those windows very often since it doesn't cool down much at night.

"I know that you got all the necessary shots before you came, but it's still a good idea to sleep under a mosquito net and use insect repellent during the day."

"Have you ever gotten malaria, Rosemary?"

"No, but I contracted dengue fever a couple of years ago, and I never want to go through that again! I had a headache and a rash for over a week," she answered. "The painful joints and fatigue lasted about six weeks, and mine wasn't even a severe case.

"I'll leave you to freshen up and get organized," she said, turning toward the kitchen. "Come on out when you're ready."

When I appeared at the kitchen door, a Haitian woman was preparing our meal.

"*Bonswa*," I said, using one of the only Creole phrases I knew.

"This is Nadia," Rosemary said to me. "She does the cooking for us so that we are free to take care of other responsibilities."

"*Nadia, se mis Pat,*" she nodded in my direction.

"*Bonswa*," Nadia said, smiling. "*Byenveni a Ayiti.*"

"Come and sit down, and I'll say grace," Rosemary said, reaching for my hand.

"Lord, I ask your presence with Pat. She's made quite a leap of faith coming so far to work with me here. Give her strength and wisdom as she makes this adjustment. Bless this food and the hands that prepared it. We ask this in Christ's name. Amen."

Nadia had placed plates of beans and rice on the table, along with what looked like fried potatoes. When I bit into one, however, it tasted more like a banana. My face must have registered surprise.

"Those are fried plantains. Aren't they good?"

I had to agree and smiled as I motioned to Nadia that I liked her cooking.

After supper, I asked Rosemary to describe a typical day in the clinic.

"Of course every day is different, but Maurice generally hands out cards with numbers on them when people start coming about five in the morning. Often they've walked for at least an hour in order to be near the front of the line."

"How many patients do you see most days? And what kinds of medical problems do you see?" I asked.

She half-shrugged as she answered.

"We do our best to help with whatever comes to us. Usually there are about thirty patients on any given morning. Some of our most common problems are worms, diarrhea, colds, cuts, burns, and scabies.

"But the greatest problem is malnutrition because it undermines people's general health," she said, shaking her head and frowning.

It was clear the medical issues would be challenging, and I was equally concerned about how I would communicate with the patients. I knew Maurice would translate, but he might not always be available.

"Do you have any books to help me learn Creole?" I asked.

"Yes," she replied, "I set aside this paperback for you. It contains common phrases and some basic medical words that will be good places to start. And don't be afraid to try the language in the clinic. That's the best way for you to learn."

I nodded, yawning. It was starting to get dark.

"I can see you're exhausted, Pat. You'll have to adjust to going to bed and waking up early, so it's probably time to call it a day. Without electricity, no one can do much after the sun goes down."

"I'm so tired I could go to bed right now," I replied, stifling another yawn.

"Don't be surprised if you're awakened by unfamiliar sounds in the night," she said as we got up from the table. "I don't notice them anymore because I'm used to them. But you may hear voodoo drums in the distance, and often dogs get to barking, donkeys will bray, and the silly roosters will crow at any hour of the day or night."

My mind and senses had just about shut down, and my eyelids were starting to droop.

"Goodnight, Rosemary, I'll see you in the morning."

"Sleep well. I'll have a pot of coffee ready when you get up."

I lay down under my mosquito net and began to pray.

"Lord, thank you for my safe trip on the airplane and with Maurice in the jeep. I know that you are with me. Help me to do your will…"

I must have fallen asleep in the midst of my prayer because suddenly I felt the warmth of the morning sun streaming in through the window and heard the *cocorico* of the rooster welcoming the new day.

I got up and put on one of the cotton shifts I'd bought in the thrift store back home. It's going to be different wearing dresses all the time, I thought, but Rosemary had told me that it was important to dress like the Haitian women. I could hear the babbling of voices coming from the front of the clinic. I looked at my watch and was amazed to see that it was only 4:15 a.m. Rosemary had said that Haitians rise very early to begin their work before the hottest part of the day, and she was right. Since the clinic didn't open until 5:00, I took some time to read my Bible before breakfast.

Sometimes it seems that God guides me to appropriate readings in his Word. Today I opened my Bible to Psalm 96 where I read,

> "Sing unto the Lord a new song; sing to the Lord,
>   all the earth.
> Sing to the Lord, praise his name; proclaim his salvation
>   day after day.
> Declare his glory among the nations,
>   his marvelous deeds among all the peoples."

I glanced out the window of my new home and prayed,

"Lord, help me to sing a new song on my first day in this clinic even though I won't be able to talk much with the people I meet. Let my actions show that I love and care for them. I pray that I'll be able to meet their needs and deal with whatever sights I see. In Jesus' name. Amen."

Trusting that God would be with me, I headed for the kitchen where I could already smell the coffee that Rosemary had promised.

CHAPTER FIVE

"*Bonjou*, Pat," Rosemary greeted me. "How'd you sleep?"

"I didn't hear a thing until a rooster crowed this morning about 4:15," I replied. "I'm a good sleeper, and anyway I was totally wiped out last night."

I poured myself a cup of coffee from the large pot on the stove.

"This coffee smells delicious. I don't function very well until I've had my first cup."

I sat at the table in the kitchen, enjoying the taste of the sausage gravy on biscuits that Nadia had prepared.

"I didn't expect to have an American breakfast here," I said.

"Harry Devon comes in to preach at the nearby church every six weeks or so, and he always brings in some staples like canned vegetables and Bisquick. Last time he surprised us with sausage gravy. The missionary who planted that church actually lived in this house that we now occupy. You'll meet Harry on Sunday after the service."

"Well, how can I be useful in the clinic today?" I asked, finishing my coffee. "It'll be tricky since I can't talk to the people yet."

"You'll pick up the language," she assured me. "Today you can help by taking blood pressures, cleaning cuts and sores, and just showing that you care."

By 5:00 a.m. we were in the clinic where I put a blood pressure cuff on an elderly man. His pressure was an alarming 160/90, and Rosemary gave him a small envelope of medicine to take once a day. Her tone of voice indicated the importance of her instructions to him.

As he left, she shared, "One of the difficulties we face is that often patients either take too much medicine or forget to take it at all. Hopefully, that man will return in two weeks and we'll see an improvement in his BP."

Our next patient was a little boy with an eye infection. He was wearing only a dirty tee shirt.

"Here, Pat, put on some gloves and wash his face and then put some of these drops in his eye. You can handle that without my help."

While I was taking care of him, I heard a commotion outside. When I looked up, two men were carrying in a third man whose leg was wrapped with a dirty towel.

Rosemary motioned to his friends to bring him quickly to the table. "We need to look at his cut right away," she said to me.

When she removed the towel, blood gushed from his leg.

"It's a machete cut," she explained. "We get a lot of these. He's either been in a fight, or he hurt himself while cutting sugar cane."

The man lay on the table while she applied pressure to the four-inch gash until the bleeding subsided. He winced when she cleaned the wound with antiseptic. I watched her put in three or four stitches and was surprised when she challenged me to finish her work.

I hesitated since this was new territory for me. I had darned socks before, but was I up to this? I decided I should give it a try. I took the needle, sterilized it, and started sewing. It probably only took ten minutes to close the wound, but it felt much longer.

"You're okay, Pat," Rosemary praised me. "Most inexperienced people would have flinched at doing that on their first day here. You've passed your initiation!" she said with a grin.

About 11:00 a.m. we had seen our last patient, and Rosemary declared that it was time for lunch.

"This afternoon I'd like to have you walk with me about two miles up into the hills. There's a twelve year old girl who can't walk anymore for some reason. I think it's malnutrition so I've been trying to take her a peanut butter sandwich and some fruit at least three times a week. We'll do therapy on her legs and try to stimulate her muscles so they won't atrophy. Plus you'll get a close-up view of the countryside and see inside a typical Haitian home."

As we hiked up the mountain that afternoon, I was surprised at the number of women walking to unseen destinations with heavy loads on their heads. No vehicle could have traveled along the steep rutted paths. Young boys rode donkeys loaded down with stalks of sugar cane, bunches of plantains, bags of rice, or jugs of water from the community pump. Fortunately I was in pretty good condition and could keep up with Rosemary's pace.

"How did you find out about this girl?" I asked after about an hour's walk up the mountain.

"Her parents brought her to the clinic a couple of weeks ago. I told them that we would visit her occasionally with something to eat and would work on her legs and feet. Here we are," she said as we turned off the main path. This smaller path looked no different from dozens of others we had passed, yet Rosemary knew just where she was.

"*Bonswa, madanm,*" Rosemary greeted the girl's mother. "This is Miss Pat who has come to help with Savina today."

"*Bonswa. Byenveni,*" the woman said softly with a shy smile.

Turning to a girl who looked no more than ten, Rosemary gave her a peanut butter sandwich and a small sweet Haitian banana. She gave similar lunches to the other five children sitting on the packed earth floor, some with no clothes on.

What a pretty child, I thought, noticing the beads and ribbons in her hair and her straight white teeth. She was seated on the only chair in the hut.

"We'll massage her legs and feet while she eats," Rosemary said to me. "Then we'll see if she can take a few steps."

I started on one foot, rubbing and squeezing it before moving upward, while Rosemary worked on the other. Her inability to walk seemed to me a strange side effect of malnutrition.

When Savina had finished her lunch, each of us took an arm and pulled her onto her feet. Her legs wobbled at first, but finally her feet flattened out, and she managed to stay upright.

"Let's try to take a step," Rosemary said to the girl and then translated for me.

As I smiled and looked into Savina's eyes, I felt her arm tighten on mine. Obviously, she was afraid, but with a show of determination, she succeeded in moving her right foot about an inch. Her siblings looked on with big round eyes

"*Trè byen,*" Rosemary said encouragingly. "Now the other one."

After Savina had managed to take about ten steps, her face broke into a big grin. Since she was obviously worn out, Rosemary asked me to move the chair close. By now we had attracted quite a crowd of children peering curiously into the windows and door at the two white women who had come to visit. Rosemary turned to the mother and spoke rapidly in Creole.

As we started down the mountain again, she explained that she'd asked Savina's mother to do the same activities with her daughter every day until we returned early next week.

"Her mother means to follow through, but with all those other children, she may get too busy. Hopefully, she'll continue the exercises to strengthen Savina's legs."

It only took 45 minutes to get back down to the clinic.

"Thank you for inviting me to join you this afternoon," I said. "The hope on Savina's face as she took those few steps was so rewarding. This whole day just confirms that this is where I'm meant to be."

CHAPTER SIX

The next month was filled with similar days, and I gradually was able to ask people's names, how old they were, where they lived, and why they had come to the clinic. Sometimes after I treated children, I would hold one of them for a few minutes and was surprised how comfortable they were being cuddled by a stranger.

A young man who sometimes helped mornings in the clinic began coming by every evening. Since Wilby was eager to learn more English and I desperately needed to learn Creole, we were able to teach each other. I was surprised at how quickly he picked up the English phrases, but he had a head start on me.

"Tell me, Wilby, why do patients call me 'Miss Pat?' I've never been called 'Miss' before."

"That's easy. In *kreyòl*, *'mis'* means nurse, and that's what you are."

"*Mèsi, mwen konprann.* Did I say that right?"

"Yes, you understand," he said encouragingly.

Those evenings marked the beginning of a warm friendship.

One day when we saw fewer patients than usual, Rosemary asked if I'd like to go with her into Gonaïves and call home.

Since there was no telephone in our little village, we had to drive into the big city to communicate with family.

"Oh yes, I'd really like to talk with Lynn and Cheryl," I said excitedly. "They're probably just fine, but it would be good to hear it for myself."

I grabbed my daypack and we jumped into the jeep.

"Let me tell you about the telephone system in Gonaïves," she said as she drove over the bumpy mountainous roads.

"We'll go to Teleco where we'll give the operator the number we want to call. It sometimes takes three or four hours for a call to go through. That's why I suggested that we go today since we finished early."

As we approached the city, Rosemary drove on whichever side of the road had the fewest ruts and tooted the horn just like everyone else.

"Seems like there'd be lots of accidents here with so many vehicles dodging each other," I observed. "And what about the pedestrians? Don't they ever get hit?"

"Actually, I guess everyone knows to pay attention," she answered. "Maybe because we're a small village without much traffic, I've never had to treat anyone who's been hit. However, I did hear of a woman who had dozed off being bounced off the back of a tap-tap. She had head injuries and was fortunate to survive."

We pulled to a stop in front of a little storefront where a woman was selling fruit, snacks, and bottled soft drinks. I could also see dresses, skirts, shorts, and tee shirts for sale spread on the ground outside the open door.

"The Teleco is in the alley by this shop," Rosemary said. "Sometimes it's hard to hear with all the street noise, but there's no other choice. Come on, I'll show you what to do."

The operator sat at a beat-up desk in a small room with benches all around the edges. I gave her Cheryl's number, praying that I'd get to talk with one of my girls. It was about 3:30 p.m. back home, and I thought that Lynn would be out of school. If I had to wait a long time, Cheryl might be there too. I sat on a bench to study the Creole phrase book that I always carried with me.

After only an hour of trying, the operator signaled me that my call had gone through. When I got to the phone, I heard a faint voice. "Hello?"

"Hi, Lynn, it's Mom. How're you doing?"

"Mom! I can't believe it's you. Where are you? I hear horns and music and voices in the background."

"We're in Gonaïves because we don't have a phone at the clinic," I said, raising my voice to be heard over the din.

"Tell me all the news. How's school? How's it going living with Cheryl? What about the rest of the family?"

"One question at a time, Mom. School's going well. I still hope you'll make it home for graduation. Cheryl's kind of strict about when I should be home at night. She's less flexible than you. Everyone else is good, and you're going to have another grandchild! Susan and Jerry are expecting in late July, so they're excited."

"Sounds like you're all getting along fine."

Despite having to repeat myself because of the background commotion, I managed to tell her a little bit about my life this past month. Then I heard her calling to Cheryl.

"Mom's on the phone! Come talk with her."

Cheryl and I talked for a few minutes before we said goodbye.

"I'll try to call you again sometime," I said. "I love you both. Tell Lynn we'll have to see about graduation. Say hi to everyone else for me. I miss you all, but I'm doing fine."

Even though I had no doubt that this was where I was supposed to be, my family did seem very far away. I'd been so busy that I hadn't realized how much I missed them.

While Rosemary made her call, I stepped out into the alley and watched the scenes around me. So many women were carrying heavy loads on their heads, and even young girls were burdened in the same way. No wonder we often heard complaints about sore necks and headaches.

I noticed a little boy across the street who was probably about three years old. He was stark naked and terribly dirty, and I could hear him crying. No one seemed to be paying any attention to him, and I wondered where his mother was. Since I couldn't bear the sight of him all alone and so miserable, I checked for traffic and walked over to him. Would he be afraid of me? I wondered. Maybe he had never seen a white person before.

I had some peanut butter crackers in my pack which I opened as I crossed the dirt road.

"*Bonswa, ti gason,*" I said as I approached him. "Do you want a cracker?"

He hesitated and then reached for it. I sat down on a crate that happened to be nearby. When I held out another cracker, he crept a little closer. It wasn't long before he laid his head on my knee and started rubbing his fingers over the downy hair on my arm. Surely his mother or sister or brother will come looking for him, I thought, but no one did.

I wiped his nose with a tissue and threw it into an open trench already filled with trash. I hated to litter, but what was one tissue in the midst of everything else in that ditch?

Glancing up, I saw Rosemary looking for me up and down the street. When I called to her, she came over with a questioning expression on her face.

"I saw him crying and looking so forlorn," I said defensively. "Where do you suppose his mother is?"

"Who knows?" she said with a shrug. "Maybe he wandered away looking for something to eat. It's even possible that he's an orphan. He's just about asleep on your knee. Now what are you going to do with him?" she asked.

It hadn't occurred to me that I'd created a dilemma by giving this poor little guy some attention.

"I'll inquire at the shop across the street to see if she knows anything about him," she said as she threaded her way between the trucks and mopeds.

Soon she returned.

"The shopkeeper says he lives with his grandmother up the street, but he comes here every day, always naked, hungry, and crying. She often gives him a mango or a piece of bread. Sometimes he takes a nap inside her shop. She said to bring him over and she'd lay him down on a mat."

Rosemary helped me up and we walked across the road. My little burden became heavier as he snuggled closer. How I wished I could take him back with us, clean him up, and give him a good meal. I voiced my thoughts to Rosemary.

"There are probably fifty more like him in this neighborhood," she said. "We can't just whisk him away and look after him ourselves." Her apparent lack of emotion took me by surprise.

I laid him down in the relative cool of the shop, touched my fingers to my lips and placed them on his cheek, the closest I could come to a kiss. What chance does he have for a decent future? I wondered.

Thanking the shopkeeper, we climbed in the jeep and headed out of the city into the countryside where there was less noise.

"How was your phone call?" Rosemary asked.

Her question pulled me out of my reverie.

"Sorry. What did you say? I was back in Gonaïves."

"I know," Rosemary responded. "It's hard to let go of the sight of a vulnerable unattended child. It takes awhile, but sometimes you just have to develop a hard shell."

During the rest of the trip home, we were quiet, deep in our own thoughts.

"Please, God, take care of that little boy. He doesn't deserve to be so neglected. Keep him and others like him safe in your gentle arms."

CHAPTER SEVEN

One evening several months later, Wilby and I were sitting outside working on our Creole/English studies when he asked, "Do you miss your family back in the States, Miss Pat? I would miss my mother and brothers and sisters if I lived so far away. Even though my father went away and left us, I still miss him."

I had never heard him talk about his father before. I had met his mother and several of his siblings, and I'd just assumed his father was around.

"Your father doesn't live with you now, Wilby?" I asked.

A frown clouded his features.

"No, lots of fathers in Haiti have many children, but when they can't find work to feed their families, or someone casts a spell on them, sometimes they just disappear. I'd never leave my family," he said emphatically.

"Do you know where your father is now?" I asked.

He shook his head with a flicker of hurt in his eyes.

"Not for sure, but he may be in Miami. The last we heard he was on the island of Tortuga where they build boats. Haitians pay a lot to try to reach the Bahamas or Miami to find work. That way they can send money back."

"So I guess you haven't heard any more from him?" I asked.

He glanced away, his lips forming a thin line, and changed the subject.

"You still haven't answered my question, Miss Pat. Do you miss your family?"

"Yes, but I'll actually get to see them before long. My youngest daughter Lynn is graduating from high school, and I'll be going home for a month in May."

"You'll be gone for four whole weeks?" he asked with alarm. "You'll be coming back, won't you? How will I keep learning English?"

"I'm not the only one who speaks English here," I reminded him. "You can talk with Rosemary and Maurice. You could even visit the new Methodist hospital occasionally. It's only four streets away. There are American doctors and nurses over there, and there might be some other Haitians who would like to practice their English with you."

"I wouldn't feel right just showing up at the hospital," he said. "I'd need a reason to go over there, don't you think?"

I could understand why he'd feel uncomfortable about just dropping in unannounced.

"I'll talk with Rosemary to see if she can come up with a reason for you to go there. Sometimes we send them some of our patients if they are too sick for us to treat here. Perhaps you could help with transporting them. We'll see what she says."

For the first time that evening, I saw a smile on Wilby's face.

"Oh, thanks, Miss Pat. I'll keep practicing my English while you're gone, but it won't be the same without you. Do you really have to go?"

"Yes, since my husband passed away, my daughter really wants her mom there to see her graduate."

"What does that mean, 'graduate'?"

"Well, Lynn will finish high school, *lekòl segondè*, in May. There will be a ceremony where she and all her classmates will receive their diplomas. After that, she's considering becoming a nurse. She asks lots of questions about my work here in the clinic and thinks she'd like to help people when they're sick."

"She's lucky," he responded. "I had to quit school when I was eleven because we couldn't afford it anymore. I wanted to be a doctor.

"It would be so great if Haiti could be like America where all kids can go to school. If I lived in the States, I would study really hard, especially science and mathematics. I liked those subjects," he said wistfully.

By now it had become quite dark, and Wilby still needed to walk home. Fortunately the moon and stars were bright. I watched him set out on the dirt path that led up the mountainside to where he lived. I hoped that the light from the moon would be enough to keep him from stumbling on the rocks, tree roots, and other obstacles along the way. I had grown very fond of him as we'd worked together on our respective languages.

As I lay down in my little room, I replayed in my head parts of the past hour's conversation.

I had been wanting to talk with Wilby about God for some time, but how could I explain God the Father to someone whose father had abandoned him? Wilby had told me that so many Haitian fathers just take off and leave their responsibilities and families behind. How can Haitians relate to God as a loving, caring father when so many of them haven't experienced that in their own families? I wondered.

"Lord, tonight I've realized again how hard life is for young people here in Haiti. Wilby's so sincere and motivated. Please reveal your loving presence to him and look out for him. I pray that he will come to know you and Jesus as we continue our conversations. In Christ's name. Amen."

Usually I can fall asleep immediately after my nightly prayers, but that night I couldn't turn off my thoughts. Life is so difficult for most Haitians, and so many turn to voodoo to make sense of their suffering. How could the truth of God's love shine light in this darkness and overturn the superstition that permeates the culture?

Suddenly I heard a voice speaking to me.

"Pat, you're becoming a nurse, friend, and confidante to my people. Wilby trusts you. He'll be ready to hear you when the time is right. Just call on me as you did tonight, and I'll guide you."

Wow! I sat straight up in bed. I had sensed God's presence before, but never that clearly. I turned on my flashlight and reached for my Bible, wondering what passage would speak to me. Of course, I thought, as I turned to the end of Matthew's gospel and reread Jesus' "Great Commission."

> "Therefore, go and make disciples of all nations,
> baptizing them in the name of the Father and
> of the Son and of the Holy Spirit, and teaching
> them to obey everything I have commanded you.
> And surely I will be with you always, to the very
> end of the age."

"Thank you, God, for renewing my vision, helping me claim my strengths, and for giving me a heart to serve."

I put my Bible down, turned off my flashlight, and settled into bed. I could feel myself relax, knowing that God would prepare people's hearts to learn of him.

Before long, I heard the rooster crowing. It seemed as if I had just fallen asleep, but obviously it was daylight and time to get up. I could hear people walking along the road outside the clinic.

After reading my Bible, I made my way into the kitchen where Rosemary had the coffee ready.

"Good morning, Rosemary. I hope Wilby and I didn't disturb you last night. I broke the news that I'll be gone for a month in May, and he doesn't want to stop learning English while I'm gone. I suggested that he might be able to go talk with the Americans at the big hospital in the afternoons. He seemed rather shy about going over there without a legitimate reason. Do you have any idea how we could get him in the door?"

She thought for a moment before replying.

"You know, it's possible that he might be able to do some translating for them. He really has learned a lot of medical vocabulary by helping us here."

She hesitated for a few minutes before speaking again.

"I've been thinking. You'll be coming back after your daughter's graduation. Do you think you'd consider staying another year?"

It didn't take me long to answer her.

"I can't say for sure until I've been home and seen with my own eyes that my family is doing well without me. But I love working here." My memories of the previous night were still vivid. "God has given me a real sense of peace about serving here."

"Yes, you do seem well-suited to this calling. There's no doubt in my mind that God's sending me to Illinois when you were at such loose ends was all part of his plan for both of us."

"Amen to that!" I agreed warmly.

CHAPTER EIGHT

"Mom, you're actually here! It's hard to believe!" Lynn exclaimed as she and Cheryl took turns hugging me at the airport.

"I thought you'd look different after eight months in Haiti," Cheryl said, "but you haven't changed a bit."

Thinking about what I'd experienced and how differently I looked at life now, I had to laugh before I answered her.

"The changes are on the inside, girls. Living in a place where most folks don't have running water and electricity or enough clothes and shoes to wear, and where eating even once a day is a luxury, changes your perspective on what really matters. But enough about me! Tell me all about the family. How is everyone?"

"Susan's finding this pregnancy harder than when she was expecting Ruthie," Cheryl said. "In fact, the doctor suspects she might be carrying twins. But so far, he's heard only one heartbeat."

"We're all having dinner together tonight, Mom. Everyone can hardly wait to see you. Connie invited us to her place since Susan doesn't feel up to entertaining right now."

What a blessing that my stepdaughter Connie is so much a part of the family, I thought.

As Cheryl drove onto the smooth busy freeway, I couldn't help but think about the roads in Haiti pitted with potholes, ruts, and huge puddles, and crowded with pedestrians and donkeys carrying their burdens along the edge.

Connie had prepared my favorite dishes, Steve fixed delicious hamburgers on the grill, little Ruthie climbed into my lap and wanted me to read to her, and the sounds of laughter filled my heart with joy. Gosh, it's good it is to be back with my family, I thought. Too bad that Richard can't be here from California.

"How about a game of euchre?" Steve asked as the girls cleared the table and loaded the dishwasher.

"The rest of you can play," I said, "but I need to lie down and take a nap. I left the clinic at 4:00 a.m. and I'm exhausted."

Susan had had a long day too. She held her lower back and suggested,

"Hey, Mom, since you're staying with us and I'm tired too, let's head for home."

As we rode the five miles to Susan and Jerry's house, they wanted to hear more about my work in the clinic, and I asked Susan about her pregnancy. My eyes grew heavy, and I was nearly asleep as Jerry drove into the garage.

"You know where the guest room is, Mom. Feel free to take a shower and we'll talk more in the morning."

The warm water soothed my tired muscles, and before long I sank into the queen-sized bed and pulled the covers around my shoulders.

"Thank you, Lord, for the blessings of my wonderful family, and for getting me here safely to see Lynn graduate. In Christ's name."

Friday night a week later I was overwhelmed when Lynn came to Susan's house, looking lovely in a beautiful lacy white dress.

"Honey, I'm so glad to be here on your special night. It's hard to believe how grown up you look. How I wish your dad were here. He'd be so proud of you." I had a lump in my throat as I thought of what Bob was missing.

When we were seated in the high school auditorium, I studied the graduation program and realized that Lynn was near the top of her class! No one had told me that she would be giving one of the speeches. The title, according to the program, was "Special People in our Lives."

"All of us are grateful tonight for certain people who have touched and guided us throughout our years in school. Tonight I'd like to pay tribute to several teachers, my pastor, and to my mother and sister. Sometimes it's hard for us to tell people how much we love and respect them, but what more appropriate time than when we're finishing one chapter and beginning the next one in the book of our lives."

I listened proudly as she mentioned her third-grade teacher who had built her self-confidence, her high school English teacher who had praised her writing abilities, and her counselor who had helped her through her grief when her father died. She went on to acknowledge her youth pastor who had led retreats that increased her faith and had encouraged her to apply to Midwest Christian College.

"Finally, I want to pay tribute to my mom, the most selfless person I've ever known. A year and a half ago when my dad died, Mom became a single parent. She'd worked for years at Lutheran Care Center where she gave the residents loving attention. Then last summer, she surprised us all by going to work in a clinic in a remote area of Haiti.

"It was hard for me to have her so far away during my senior year, but now I realize that she had already prepared me to be capable and self-sufficient. She felt called by God to care for and nurse people who have to struggle for the basic things in life that we take for granted.

"Realizing that I needed someone who would be responsible for me, Mom asked my next older sister to take me in. Cheryl was only twenty-one at the time, but she supported and loved me during this year, and I want her to know how grateful I am."

I glanced at Cheryl who was wiping tears away as she listened to her younger sister's appreciative words.

Lynn then turned to her fellow students on the stage and spoke directly to them.

"I challenge all of you to share your gratitude with those who have been important to you. Write a note to your favorite teachers. Thank your grandparents and parents for specific times when they've been there for you. You know who has influenced you positively. Let them know that they made a difference in your life.

"Finally, reach out to someone such as a family member, an elderly neighbor, a disabled friend, or anyone you see who needs a word of encouragement. When we reach out, we're passing on the legacy of those who helped us.

"Thank you," she concluded.

At first, everyone was quiet, and then her classmates stood and began to applaud. Soon the entire audience was on their feet as Lynn returned to her seat. I thought my heart would burst with pride at the maturity and self-assurance of my youngest daughter.

During the rest of my month's furlough, I spent time with each of my children. Lynn and I went shopping to get what she'd need for college. I also visited the nursing home and learned that my dear Nora had died.

A few days before I returned to Haiti, Lynn and I decided to take a day just for fun.

"Let's drive over to St. Louis and see some of the sights," she said. "That will give us lots of time in the car to visit, and we can have lunch in the city and still get back by dark."

"I like that idea," I said. "I haven't seen the view from the top of the Arch in years. You were about ten years old when your dad and I took you and Cheryl over there."

We left the next morning.

"So how does it feel to be going away to college?" I asked as we passed the exit off I-70 that leads to Midwest Christian.

"It's exciting and scary both," she said. "I'm glad it's a small Christian college instead of a big state university. I can't imagine being one of several thousand freshmen. I'm also glad that Jenny will be going to Midwest and be my roommate. And it really helps that her parents are renting a U-Haul so we can both take all our stuff at one time."

"That's a relief to me too since I won't be here to help you get situated. It's a good thing you can handle change as well as you do. I'm really proud of you, you know."

She was quiet for a few minutes.

"You know, Mom, even though Jenny and I are good friends, sometimes I wonder if she'll ever grow up. She's awfully dependent because her mom has always been so overprotective. After Dad died, with you having to work such long hours to support us, we had to figure out how to take care of ourselves. By your example, you helped us learn to make good decisions, handle our money wisely, and think before we acted impulsively. I meant what I said in my graduation speech about how much I appreciate and love you.

"It was tough at first when you left to go to Haiti last year," she continued. "There were times when I really missed our late night talks, but Cheryl and I became very close after awhile. When Joe and I broke up last January, she listened when I was upset and helped me see that maybe breaking up was for the best."

"I'm glad you had Cheryl to lean on. What you said about her at graduation meant a lot to her."

"I wish it were easier to keep in touch with you when you're gone, Mom," she said. "It's hard to imagine not having electricity or phone service at the clinic. I'd like to be able to call and just talk whenever I want to. Even though you've shared a lot during this visit home, I can't really picture a whole country where most people don't have phones, or indoor plumbing, or safe water to drink."

Her comments illustrated how hard it is for Americans to understand the lives of people in so-called third world countries. In fact, Wilby had told me that many Haitians consider Haiti a fourth world country, so great are their challenges and problems. After all, they had been exploited for centuries first by the Spaniards, then by the French, and most recently by the notorious dictators "Papa Doc" and "Baby Doc" Duvalier. By the time Haiti gained its independence in 1804, most of its resources had been depleted, and the population of former slaves lacked education and leadership.

"You know, Lynn, the people of Haiti are proud to be the first black democracy in this hemisphere, but they were 'in the hole' before they ever had a chance to thrive. Spain and France both had colonies in Haiti and plundered its riches, and early on, the U.S. kept its distance because it had only been around for about thirty years itself and was still very reliant on slave labor."

I felt my stomach knot with emotion.

"From what I can tell, 'Baby Doc' is no better than his father. These past thirty years, the Duvaliers just lined their pockets and promoted voodoo as a way of controlling the people. Neither father nor son did anything to prevent thousands of their citizens from dying of hunger or disease, and hundreds more were murdered for opposing them. Rosemary and I just try to avoid politics and do our work without attracting attention."

Lynn clearly sensed the intensity of my feelings.

"Do you ever wonder whether what you're doing is worth it, Mom? It sounds so overwhelming. I'd think sometimes you'd want to give up."

"Occasionally it does get to me. To tell you the truth, there are days when I'd just like to pack up and clear out. But then God gives me peace. I love the Haitian people. They are friendly and strong and resilient, and they're so grateful for the help we give them. Like holding a child, for example. It is such a small thing that means so much. I see parents who love their kids fiercely, but they are always scrambling to figure out how to care for them and feed so many mouths. So that bit of attention I can provide really feels like Jesus is hugging them through me."

I told her about Savina and how we'd helped her with food and taught her mom how to work with her so she could walk again.

"Each time we see improvement like that, it makes all our efforts worthwhile. If you could spend time with Wilby, the young man who's teaching me Creole, you'd see why these people have become so dear to me. I miss being with them and I'm ready to go back, though it's certainly been good to be home with all of you."

We enjoyed the view of the Mississippi River from the windows at the top of the Arch, had lunch at a café on the river, and did some shopping downtown before heading home again. In a bookstore I found a journal with quotes from the Bible that I bought to take to Rosemary. She often recorded events of the day and her feelings about the people she served.

Lynn fell asleep in the car as we started home. When we stopped for supper, she said, "Thanks, Mom, for spending today with me," as we slid into a booth. "I think maybe we're closer than a lot of moms and daughters who see each other all the time."

"You're right, honey. I'll treasure the memory of this day with you."

After finishing our hamburgers, I put my arm around Lynn's shoulders as we went out the door.

"I'll be praying that you'll have a successful first year in college, that you'll make good friends, and that you will find the direction God wants for your future."

"Thanks, Mom, I'll be praying for you too," and we got back in the car for the rest of our ride home.

CHAPTER NINE

"Pat, we've missed you so much! When patients come for follow-up visits, they always ask about you and want to know when you'll back," Rosemary said, giving me a big hug.

Bringing my suitcase in from the jeep, Maurice said, "I told her on the way how excited Wilby is about seeing her today. In fact, isn't that him coming from the hospital right now?"

I looked down the road, and sure enough, Wilby was running toward the clinic with a big grin on his face.

When he reached the doorway, he rushed inside, grabbed me by the waist and swung me around.

"Put me down, you silly boy," I said, laughing and hugging him at the same time.

He stopped twirling me around and stood back, as if he couldn't believe it was really me.

"I'm so glad you're back. Can we talk tonight?" he asked eagerly.

"Maybe for a short while. The trip wore me out, but I do want to hear about your work at the hospital," I said. "You'll have to let me practice my Creole too."

"Okay, I'll see you tonight," he said as he waved good-bye and headed back to the hospital.

I had a quick bite to eat and went to my room to grab a short nap. No sooner had I closed my eyes than Rosemary came to find me.

"Pat, wake up! You'll never guess who's just showed up on our doorstep."

Shaking the cobwebs from my head, I made my way to the clinic.

I couldn't believe my eyes when I looked at the boy sitting on our exam table. It was the little three-year-old from Gonaïves that I had held while Rosemary was on the phone several weeks earlier. The shopkeeper was standing next to him.

"He seemed very hot, and I didn't know what to do for him," she said in Creole, which I could still understand after a month's absence. "When he kept crying and pulling on his ear, I knew he needed help, but I can't afford a doctor."

"I'm surprised it was you who brought him to us. Didn't you say he lives with his grandmother?" I asked the shopkeeper.

The woman looked down at him sadly.

"His grandmother died recently. When I noticed his ear was bothering him, I remembered you. He cried all the way here on the tap-tap."

"Let me hold him," I said, reaching out to him. "He liked that the other time."

Sure enough, when I picked him up, he reached his arms around my neck, laid his head on my shoulder, and stopped crying. I sat in the rocker which Maurice had made for our clinic and started singing "Jesus Loves Me" as we rocked back and forth.

"I'll heat some water, Pat, so you can wash his face before we look at his ear," Rosemary said. "Fortunately, we just received a shipment of antibiotics which should clear up the infection."

As I cleaned him up, I recognized from his distended belly and his pale thinning hair that he was in stage three malnutrition. Poor little guy, I thought, what's going to happen to him now?

He looked up at me with feverish brown eyes and kept tugging on his ear. I was heartsick at the thought that he was now an orphan.

We gave him some children's Tylenol for the pain and an injection of an antibiotic. But when I held a week's supply of Tylenol out to the shopkeeper, she put her hands up, backed away, and shook her head.

"I can't take him home. I have seven children of my own, and I have to run my shop. Can't you keep him here?" she pleaded.

Rosemary and I looked at each other.

"How about if I keep him with me in my room until he gets better?" I offered. "In the meantime we could pray that we find someone to take him in."

Rosemary smiled indulgently.

"I had a feeling you were going to come up with something like that, but we can't start doing this on a regular basis. God help us, it's going to be a real challenge to find a home for him."

The shopkeeper was obviously anxious to leave.

"I have to get back to my family and store," she said, edging toward the door.

She squeezed the little guy's hand affectionately and hurried out into the street. As I watched her climb onto the back of a moped, I thanked God for sending this Good Samaritan.

I went to the kitchen where I found my little friend some leftover rice and half a banana. Returning to the clinic, I picked him up and sat down in the rocking chair to feed him. His temperature was still high, but he managed to eat a few small bites. When he dozed off a few minutes later, I laid him on a blanket in the corner.

"I wonder what his name is," I said to Rosemary as we tiptoed out of the room. "I think I'll just call him 'Timoun' for now since that means little person."

That evening Wilby and I sat in our usual spot taking turns conversing in Creole and English. I was impressed by the improvement in his English and his excitement about translating at the hospital. I told him about Timoun and how we needed to find a home for him.

"That's not going to be easy. Most families already have many children to feed," he said. "There are six kids in my family plus my grandma who isn't well. My mother has enough people to care for. It's the same way for my aunts."

"Rosemary isn't sure we should have kept him," I admitted, "but we really didn't have much choice. He didn't have anyone else."

That night, as I lay in bed, I realized that only God could solve this problem.

"Lord," I prayed, "you sent this little boy to us today, knowing that he's sick and all alone in the world. I know that you love your children and I ask that you'll help us find Timoun a home. In the name of your Son who said, 'Let the little children come to me.'"

CHAPTER TEN

"Well, Pat, what have you decided about staying on for another year?" Rosemary asked one Saturday morning in mid-September. "You're willing to tackle whatever comes your way, and I've come to depend on you."

"I love it here. Unless you tell me you don't need me anymore, there's no way I'm leaving.

"By the way," I continued, "I have a lead on a potential family for Timoun. When Wilby and I were talking last night, he said that one of the Haitian nurses at the hospital has a friend who can't have children. She might be willing to take him in. Wouldn't that be great? I think God is answering our prayers."

Just then there was a tap at the door. We were surprised to see a nun standing in the opening.

"May I come in?" she asked in simple Creole with what might have been a French accent.

"I'm from the Catholic clinic on the west side of town," she explained. "Yesterday a mother brought in a child with a bad case of scabies, and we didn't have the necessary medicine. We were hoping that you might have some that you could spare."

"I didn't even know that there was a clinic across town. How long has it been in existence?" Rosemary inquired.

"We're very new. A small group of nuns from France came a month ago after a priest reported the terrible need here in the Artibonite region."

"This may be a real godsend," Rosemary remarked. "We have the medicine you need, but we're out of quinine right now. Perhaps we can help each other."

"We'd be happy to share supplies from time to time," the nun responded.

"By the way, I'm Rosemary Austin and this is my assistant Pat Hamilton."

"And I'm Soeur Marie-Élisabeth," she said, shaking our hands.

We chatted for a few more minutes before she said, "Well, I'd better be getting back." Rosemary handed her a bottle of Benedryl and some steroid cream which she tucked into her bag.

"Thank you. Please come over and visit us soon."

As the nun started back, Rosemary turned to me and said, "It's good to know that there's another clinic we can work with. Sometimes I feel as if we're in competition with the hospital here rather than working cooperatively. I like her attitude."

That evening when Wilby came by, he brought a Haitian woman of perhaps twenty-three or twenty-four with him.

"I want you to meet Lowanda, the friend of the nurse at the hospital," he said. Then turning to her, he said in Creole, "This is Miss Rosemary, and over here with Timoun in her lap is Miss Pat."

The young woman shyly walked over to me and knelt down beside the rocking chair. She reached out and gently stroked Timoun's cheek with her finger, and he clasped it in his hand. How far he had come since the shopkeeper brought him here a month ago. His ear infection was gone, he had gained four pounds, and his hair was growing back in.

"Can I hold him?" she asked softly.

"If he'll let you," Rosemary said. "He's pretty attached to Miss Pat, but he seems to like you."

I stood up, and Lowanda stretched out her arms. I hoped I hadn't spoiled him so much that he wouldn't go to her.

His lip quivered and he buried his face in my shoulder. She moved behind me and began to sing a Haitian lullaby, which he seemed to recognize. Perhaps his grandmother had sung it to him. When Lowanda reached for him again, he went to her willingly, and she sat down to rock him.

Wow, I thought, for a woman without children, she certainly knows how to win them over. As I watched them, I noticed that he was no longer sitting up straight but had snuggled down close to her, and his eyes were drooping.

"Thank you, God," I said silently. "You've performed another miracle for both Lowanda and Timoun."

"Do you think I could take him home tonight?" she asked.

I looked at Rosemary, sensing he needed more time.

As if reading my thoughts, she suggested, "Let's have you come by a few times so that he can get used to you. Then you could take him to your house for a couple of short visits so your husband can meet him. In a week or so, I expect he'll be ready to move in with you."

"That will help me adjust to his leaving too," I added. "It will be good for him to have you for his mother, but I'm really going to miss him."

Over the next four years, my life centered around the clinic most of the time. About once a year, I went on furlough and visited my family back in Illinois. On my second visit home, I met my new little grandson who filled my lap and heart. Susan hadn't been expecting twins after all.

Lynn had earned an Associate degree at Midwest Christian and had completed a one-year nursing program. After graduating, she had found a position working on the pediatric floor at the regional hospital outside Ramsey.

One Sunday when we were all gathered at Susan's, I asked Lynn,

"Could I come by the hospital to visit one day? Do you think they'd let me observe you with the children?"

"I think so, but I'll have to ask," she said. "I'd like that."

A few days later I had permission to shadow Lynn as she made her rounds and gave the children their medications. She obviously loved her work and was good at it.

As we were eating lunch in the cafeteria that day, I said, "Lynn, I'm so pleased that you chose to go into nursing. I wish I had the professional training you have."

"But Mom, you have a natural way with people, and you've learned from experience how to treat basic medical needs. You should feel good about what you're doing."

"Most of the time I feel adequate, but there are times when I'd be lost without Rosemary's expertise. However, we're not very busy these days, and we're worried that the hospital is going to put us out of business. I don't know what I'll do if that happens."

"Oh, Mom, you've invested so much time and energy in that clinic. It would be a real shame if Rosemary had to close down.

"I expect there'd always be a place for your services at Lutheran Care Center," she said.

I secretly wondered if I'd still find working in a nursing home satisfying, but I didn't mention my doubts to Lynn. I'd come to love the Haitian people, and I dreaded the thought of no longer working with them.

As we took our trays over to the counter, Lynn bumped elbows with a young male nurse about her age.

"Hi Phil," she said cheerily. "This is my mom."

"Glad to meet you, Mrs. Hamilton. I've heard a lot about you," he said with a smile.

"He seems nice," I said to Lynn as he turned to leave.

"Yes, he is," she answered, blushing slightly.

Soon after I returned to Marchand Dessalines, Rosemary broke the anticipated news that she would have to close the clinic. A few loyal patients continued to come to us for medical care, but the hospital could provide services that were beyond our scope.

"But what will you do, Rosemary?" I inquired. "You've been here a long time, and the people love you."

"I'm going to join the nuns at the Catholic clinic. They're far enough from the hospital that they're much busier than we are. I wish they had room for the two of us, but they don't."

"I'm glad you'll get to stay here, Rosemary. I guess God has other plans for me."

Over the course of the next week, I helped Rosemary pack our supplies so that she could move things across town to the Catholic clinic. After she padlocked the door, she hugged me warmly and climbed into the jeep with Maurice.

"Thank you, Pat, for being my right-hand person for five years. When I asked you to join me, I had no idea what a blessing you would be and certainly had no thoughts that we would have to close our doors. God bless you as you seek to follow his call in the future, wherever you may go."

We both cried wondering whether our paths would ever cross again. I waved as the jeep disappeared in the dust. Wilby and I were left standing alone. He and I were going to walk to Lowanda's to say good-bye before Maurice returned to take me to the airport.

"Miss Pat, I'll never forget you. Thank you for teaching me English, for getting me started at the hospital, and for telling me about God's love for us Haitians. I know he has a plan for you, even though you don't know what it is."

"Wilby, I will pray for God to bless and keep you in the years ahead. You've been like a son to me, and I'll always remember our time together. Now we'd better get ourselves over to Lowanda's," I said, turning for a last look at the clinic.

Wilby grabbed my suitcases and we began our short walk. Timoun was nearly seven now and getting tall and handsome. He was playing jacks on the hard swept dirt in front of his house when he saw me coming and raced toward me. He took my hand and led me to his home.

Lowanda gave us a warm welcome and brought out some white plastic chairs so we could sit down. Timoun hovered close by, having seen my suitcases and sensing that this visit was different.

"Miss Pat, I want to talk to you about something before you leave. Now that Timoun is so much bigger, I think he ought to have a real name instead of 'little person.' That just doesn't seem to fit him anymore. I'd like to call him Roland after my father. How would you feel about that?" she asked.

"Since he's your child now, Lowanda, it's your decision, but I do like that name. I'm happy that he has such a good home, and I'm sorry that I won't be around to see him grow up."

"You really do have to leave, don't you?" Lowanda said sadly. "Timoun will miss you. Can I say a prayer for you before you go?"

The four of us stood and held hands.

"Dear God," Lowanda began with heartfelt emotion, "Thank you for bringing my friend Miss Pat here. She helped people when they were sick, she taught us to love you and Jesus, and thanks to her, my husband and I have a son. *Mèsi Jezi!* Please God, give her a safe journey home and help her find another place to serve. Amen."

Tears were running down my cheeks as I reached out to her and Timoun for a final hug. I was too choked up to say anything other than "Thank you, I love you both, and God bless you" before I went outside where Maurice was waiting.

CHAPTER ELEVEN

As Lynn had predicted, Miss Spence at Lutheran Care Center was glad to hire me back. During the five years I'd been away, many of the residents like Nora had died, but others had moved in, keeping the place full.

I bathed and dressed people, fed those who couldn't feed themselves, pushed wheelchairs, and visited the lonely. Yet I didn't find the same kind of satisfaction that I had felt while serving in Haiti.

"I don't understand how I used to be perfectly happy working at the Care Center for sixteen years, but these days I feel restless and don't look forward to going to work," I said to my sister Enid one evening at her home.

"It's probably because you've changed, Pat. I've never been to Haiti, but from what you've told me, the needs there are so great that whatever you can do to help makes an enormous difference."

I thought about little Timoun and realized that more than likely he wouldn't be alive if I hadn't noticed him that day after my telephone call. Enid had really put her finger on what kept drawing me to Haiti. But she had more to say.

"It seems to me you have a huge heart for children that working with the elderly in the nursing home doesn't satisfy.

And sharing your faith in a place like Haiti that is so in need of hope must be deeply fulfilling. I can understand your restlessness. But for now, I think you should enjoy the time with your family back here," she advised. "Surely another door to Haiti will open for you in God's time, if it's his will."

"You and I used to have such different priorities and interests, Enid. I didn't expect you to be able to put words to my feelings. I hope you're right about God's plans for me."

During my first months back, I lived with Susan and Jerry in their large farmhouse. One evening after supper while Susan was out, Jerry and I sat down on the porch after putting the children to bed.

"Do you feel like having a cup of coffee, Mom?" Jerry asked. "I could use some advice."

"Sure, I made some brownies after work today, and I'll bring a plate of those too."

Once we'd settled on the porch swing, I turned to him and said, "What's on your mind?"

"You know how you felt that God had called you to Haiti?" he began. "Well, I keep getting messages that he wants me to be a minister. I don't mean that he actually tells me that, but things keep happening that are leading me to consider it."

"What kinds of things, Jerry?" I asked.

"Well, last week I went to visit Helen Evans in the hospital. She's struggling with liver cancer, and I've known her since I was a kid. We talked about the old days, and then she asked me to pray with her. I wasn't sure what I'd say, but the words just started flowing. It was as if God was telling me what she needed to hear."

"That does sound like God's voice," I agreed, reaching for a brownie. "Anything else that's pointing you toward the ministry?"

"Yes, Pastor Bill has been having trouble finding enough people to fill the pulpit for him next month when he goes on vacation. He approached me yesterday and invited me to bring the message on the second Sunday of the month. I've never preached before, but it would be challenging to study the scripture and open myself to God's leading. Do you think I could do it?" he asked.

"I'm sure you could deliver an inspiring sermon, Jerry. However there's a lot more to being a good pastor than preaching and visiting people in the hospital. But if you continue to feel this way, I say go for it. It will be important to have Susan behind this idea, though, both with the challenges of seminary and afterwards as a minister."

"You're right, Mom, and that may be a problem," he said.

"What do you mean?" I asked.

He hesitated for a moment, choosing his words.

"Susan and I aren't making a very good living here on the farm. The price of milk has dropped so much lately that we're considering selling the cows. Susan is pushing me to send out my resumé to companies here in town.

"Recently, I tried to talk with her about feeling called to the ministry. I was stunned by her negative reaction. She stated in no uncertain terms that she hadn't signed on to be a minister's wife. She figured she'd be obligated to help run the church and be involved in all the activities. Even though her faith is a vital part of her life, she doesn't want to feel trapped by a bunch of church people's expectations."

I could understand my daughter's feelings, but I also could see how important this was to Jerry. Still they would have a lot of hurdles to overcome.

"Sometimes it's hard to separate our will from God's, isn't it?" I observed.

"I assume you've considered the financial aspects. You know how expensive Bible College is. You'd have to get a part-time job, wouldn't you?"

"We'd have the money from the sale of the cows, and I expect I could find work with flexible hours. It's just that I don't see how we'd weather the struggles ahead without Susan's backing," he said with a sigh.

"It's obvious you feel strongly that you're hearing God's call. I remember that's how I felt before I went to Haiti. I'd like to be going back there now, but I don't know how or where I'd serve. Enid says that God will open a door for me and give me direction. Perhaps the same thing applies to you if you don't get too impatient."

"Thanks for listening, Mom. I appreciate your wisdom. I'll keep asking for God's direction for both Susan and me."

"Good night, Jerry," I said as he went inside. "I'll pray about it also." I stayed outside in the cool night air reflecting on how the Spirit works in people's lives.

A few minutes later the phone rang, and soon Jerry called to me.

"It's your sister Enid. She has an invitation for you."

"Hi there," I said when I got to the phone. "What's going on?"

"I just learned that Larry Owen from Northwest Haiti Christian Mission will be speaking at the opening session of the missionary conference in Peoria next Sunday night. He's probably just looking for money the way missionaries have to, but maybe this is the open door that we talked about. Do you want to go?"

"That's amazing. Jerry and I were just talking about ways God gives us direction and you called with this news of this conference. Do you know where this Northwest Haiti Christian Mission is?"

"Not specifically," she answered, "but I know it's further north than where you were before. We'll find out soon enough."

When Sunday arrived and Enid picked me up, I was eager to hear about this mission.

After the opening worship service of the convention, Larry Owen was introduced. He was the Executive Director of the mission that had been founded several years earlier on the northern coast of Haiti, in the town of St. Louis du Nord.

As he described the vision and goals of the mission, I felt myself getting really excited.

"God is doing great things in northwest Haiti, my friends. In the poorest part of the poorest nation in the whole Western Hemisphere, He has given me a vision to feed the children and show them the love of Jesus. Those who respond to His call become the hands and feet of our Savior, for it is through us that people see how much God loves them. As we clothe the naked, feed the hungry, tend the sick, and comfort the brokenhearted, we bring them the Good News of new life in Christ.

"We employ a fine Christian midwife named Magdala who goes to people's homes when babies are due. Without medical attention, childbirth in our region results in the death of either the mother or the child about half the time.

"Through Magdala, we've identified a number of severely malnourished children whose mothers are desperate to save them. I'm here tonight to appeal for your help. I need someone to organize and run a feeding program for these little children. The physical, spiritual, economic, and social poverty is heart wrenching, and our workers are stretched thin. I believe that God is calling someone in this very room to take on this responsibility for at least a couple of years."

I scarcely heard the rest of his address. Was this the opportunity I'd been looking for? I wondered. I had more experience running a clinic, but if leading a feeding program was what Larry needed, I could probably do that. I decided to seek him out at the end of the evening while Enid went to explore the displays lining the walls of the convention center.

I had to wait since several others were lined up to ask questions and speak with him. I could hear him talking finances with the person ahead of me.

When it was my turn, I decided to be direct.

"I'd like to volunteer to go to your mission and run your feeding program," I said. "I spent five years in Marchand Dessalines until the clinic there closed, and I can't get Haiti out of my mind. I grew to love the people, especially the children, and I miss being with them."

"Hmm," he said, rubbing his beard. "I hadn't really expected a woman to be interested in running the program. Haiti is a difficult place since it doesn't have the creature comforts that Americans are accustomed to. On the other hand, you've spent five years there and are acquainted with the difficulties. Are you sure this is what you want to do?"

"I'm positive. Ever since the clinic in Marchand Dessalines closed and I returned home, I've been restless, wanting to go back. I've been praying for an opening where I'm needed, and I think God has just placed it in my lap!"

"How does your family feel about your leaving again?" he asked.

"I've talked to them repeatedly about it, and they're behind me. My youngest daughter is twenty-three and a pediatric nurse. All of my kids are self-sufficient now."

It was hard to tell from his expression if he was sure I was the one he was looking for.

"I'm going to give you a couple of days to think about this," he said. "Pray about it, and then you can call and let me know. Here's my phone number in Kentucky. I'll be returning to Haiti at the end of the week, and you're welcome to go with me if you can get ready that fast and are convinced it's what God is calling you to do."

Although I did pray, I didn't have to consider it long. As soon as I called Larry and we made travel arrangements, I began packing and visiting my family to say good-bye once again. This time, leaving was much easier since they understood and everyone was grown up.

I did need to talk with Susan, however, about Jerry's wanting to be a minister, and I had a chance one evening when he was at a meeting. After saying goodnight to the children, she suggested sitting on the porch. That seemed to be everyone's favorite place to relax and talk.

"Mom, I hope this new calling will give you a sense of fulfillment. I'm glad that God has provided this new direction for you. As always, we'll miss you. The kids have really enjoyed having you around this time."

"I'll miss you too, but you don't really need me here. You are all capable of handling your own lives. But Jerry tells me that you're struggling to make ends meet here on the farm and that your family may be facing some major changes."

"Yes, you're right," she said with a frown and a big sigh. "Did he tell you what else he's thinking about?"

I nodded and tried to choose my next words carefully.

"He mentioned that he's feeling a call to go into the ministry. Since that would involve going to Bible College, you would both be dealing with a lot of change."

"That's for sure, and I'm not very happy with the idea of being a minister's wife," she said. "You know that church members think they're hiring both the minister and his wife. I like staying home with my kids, and I can't see myself being tied down to women's meetings, teaching Sunday School, singing in the choir, and everything else that would be expected of me. Just look at Pastor Bill's wife. She seems happy to be his right-hand person, but that's not for me."

"I think things may be changing in that respect. Pastor Bill and his wife are of a different generation. Perhaps you could have more freedom to be yourself than you think."

"Do you want another cup of coffee, Mom?" she asked rather abruptly. "I'm going inside for one."

I hoped she hadn't gone inside thinking I'd stuck my nose in where it didn't belong.

When she returned with more coffee, I was pleased to see a tentative smile on her face.

"Perhaps you're right. Maybe Jerry and I should have another talk. Thanks for helping me see some other possibilities."

The next day I turned in my resignation at the care center and apologized for not giving two weeks notice. Miss Spence seemed to understand and wished me well.

"We always appreciate your efforts with our residents, Pat. If things don't work out, you're welcome to return here."

As I shook her hand and thanked her, I felt sure that my place was in Haiti. I could hardly wait to get started.

CHAPTER TWELVE

I flew to Miami on Saturday morning where Larry met me at the airport, and we waited together for an afternoon flight into Port-au-Prince. It was nearly sunset as we flew into the capital city, and the mountains on my left and the vast ocean on my right were stunningly beautiful. That night, I could see the whole Milky Way, and there was a full moon,

After staying overnight at a hotel in Port-au-Prince, we were up and boarding the bus at 4:00 a.m. for the small rural town of St. Louis du Nord. Even though we were the only *blancs* on the public bus, I felt welcomed by the warm smiles and the nodded "*bonjou*" greetings of our fellow passengers.

I recalled the trips to Gonaïves over the potholes and ruts in the clinic's jeep. This bus ride seemed even bumpier, and just as we left Gonaïves, one of the tires went flat. We stood around in the boiling hot sun for about fifteen minutes before the tire was changed and we could get back on the bus and be on our way.

If I thought the road to Gonaïves was bad, it became even worse the further north we went. I felt fortunate to be seated near the front of the bus.

"We'll get there soon if the Big River isn't flooded," Larry commented, noticing my greenish pallor.

"Oh Lord, please don't let this trip last much longer," I prayed. "I'm pretty tough, but this ride is definitely getting to me."

Soon we stopped for gas in Port-de-Paix, which gave us a chance to get out, walk around, and buy a watermelon-mango soda from a street vendor. The main roads in this city had been paved, and for a while the ride was much smoother.

"We're only about eight miles from St. Louis, but with all the mud and deep puddles, it will take nearly an hour," Larry said.

We traveled past what had once been a harbor but now looked like a graveyard for boats. One of them was aground and nearly broken in two. As we came to La Pointe, Larry pointed out the local Haitian hospital.

"Sometimes we have to send patients there for surgery." Larry explained.

Before long I saw a double concrete archway over the road with the words, "*Bienvenue à St. Louis du Nord.*"

"I'm always glad to see that sign," Larry said, "because it means that we've arrived in St. Louis. We still have to get up the hill to the mission, but we'll catch a tap-tap for that final leg."

A few minutes later a colorfully painted pickup came along with its radio blaring. We piled into the back with our luggage, and the driver took us past the huge Catholic Church, made a sharp right turn, and drove us up a terribly steep hill. After that, the rest of the dirt road was comparatively smooth, and we soon arrived at the black iron gate that marked the entrance to the Northwest Haiti Christian Mission. We jumped down, grabbed our suitcases, and went into the large concrete building that would be my home for the years ahead.

"This will be your room," Larry said, "and hopefully someone will have rice and beans ready for us to eat before we settle in for the night."

I washed my face, made up my bed, and decided to lie down for a brief nap, even though the room was swelteringly hot. I figured that I could pull my cot outside under the stars if it didn't cool down later in the evening.

Despite the heat, I fell asleep and didn't awaken until I heard a loud *cocorico* from a rooster greeting the morning sun. I couldn't believe I'd slept ten hours straight.

"You missed supper," Larry teased me when I found the kitchen. "You must be starved. Have a cup of coffee. I'm making oatmeal."

After breakfast, Larry showed me around and introduced me to Magdala who rewarded me with a big smile when I greeted her in Creole. We immediately got to work brainstorming ideas for getting the feeding program underway. Already I had a peace in my heart that it was God's leading that had brought me back to Haiti.

We started by providing mothers with enough rice and beans for one meal a day for the children in the program. But over the next few weeks, I realized we needed to change from a rice and beans give-away to a more secure set-up. Sometimes families would be robbed of their food before they ever made it home. Others would sell it to buy tobacco and alcohol. Surely there had to be better way, I thought.

I decided that the best solution would be to provide cooked food for the children to eat on-site at the mission. I started cooking morning meals for about twelve severely malnourished children, but within two weeks we had twenty-five coming on a daily basis.

Sometimes if they had a cold, I'd give them some cold medicine. It wasn't long before I'd hear, "My mom is sick," or "My dad is sick," or "My grandpa is sick. Can he come see you?" I just couldn't refuse as they looked at me with their big brown eyes, and so began the clinic. It would soon grow to be an integral part of our ministry in St Louis.

One toddler showed up each morning with no clothes on. I would dress and feed him every day, and he actually began to get pretty fat. One Saturday he fell off a couch, and it appeared he'd broken his arm. I found a flat piece of wood and fashioned a splint to protect it.

"Oh, Navius," I said, picking him up and wiping his tears. "We need to get you to the hospital in La Pointe, but that'll have to wait until after the weekend."

On Monday we learned that no one would be there to take an x-ray before Wednesday. I continued to give him children's Tylenol, fed him rice and beans, and tried to make him comfortable. He slept on a cot in my room where I could keep an eye on him.

When a doctor finally got around to seeing us, he confirmed that the arm was indeed broken. On the way home, we stopped in to update the aunt with whom Navius lived.

"Madame Pierre, little Navius has a broken arm. Would you mind if he stayed with me for a few weeks while his arm is healing? He can still come to the feeding program, I'll make sure he gets his medicine, and you'd be able to see him anytime you want."

"Miss Pat, God has heard my prayer. I have too many children of my own to feed, and I'm grateful that you want to help my nephew."

From that time on, Navius stayed at the mission. Before long I considered him my unofficially adopted son.

CHAPTER THIRTEEN

About a year later, Larry came up to me in the courtyard.

"Pat, I want you to walk downtown with me this afternoon. I've noticed that an awful lot of *gran moun* (elderly people) are looking malnourished. We need to talk with them to see if my hunch is right."

"Of course I'll go with you, but we don't have money to feed another group or the manpower to add another program. Who do you have in mind to start an elderly feeding program?"

He grinned and winked at me.

"Don't worry. Did you think I would add a new responsibility to your already busy schedule? When I was back in the States last week, I met a couple named Dave and Vicki who are interested in serving the Lord in Haiti. They want to come right away, and they might be just right for the job."

As soon as we walked down the hill, we stopped to talk to a wizened old man sitting on a rock all by himself. His arms and legs were like sticks, and his face was full of deep wrinkles.

"*Bonswa, mesye*," Larry said. "*M' rele Larry. Kijan ou rele?*"

We learned his name was Antoine, and that he hadn't eaten in two days. We gave him a package of peanut butter crackers that he hurriedly opened.

As we started to leave, we heard him say, "*Mwen swaf.*" Larry reached into his backpack and gave him a bottle of water.

We continued our walk through the square where we made note of several other elderly men and women with the same emaciated look.

The large Catholic Church and school dominated the city square. As we crossed the plaza, I became aware of band music approaching.

"Is there some kind of celebration today?" I asked Larry.

"Look down the main street and you'll figure it out in a couple minutes," he said, removing his hat in a respectful gesture.

As we watched, a long procession of well-dressed people came around the corner. First there were men in white shirts and ties playing trombones, trumpets, saxophones and drums. Next I could see a casket being carried by young men who were all decked out in their Sunday best. They were followed by a large group of people wearing choir robes and carrying brightly colored artificial flowers. A final group of mourners was swaying and wailing loudly. Soon the entire procession made its way up the wide front steps into the church.

"Well, now you've seen a typical Haitian funeral procession," Larry said. "Somehow this family managed to find enough money to pay for a band and professional mourners. That's what all the wailing is about. After the service they'll leave the church and walk all the way to the cemetery beside the entrance arch to St. Louis."

Funerals I had seen in Marchand Dessalines weren't generally this elaborate, I thought to myself.

Leaving the square behind, we made our way through open lots strewn with piles of smoldering garbage. We dodged pigs rooting in the open ditches, skinny dogs sniffing for scraps, and naked children playing with rickety homemade wagons built from empty tin cans and plastic lids.

Before long we came upon an elderly lady squatting in the doorway of her small home. She moved in a most peculiar way, scooting along on her buttocks and hands, her knees permanently bent. Our conversation with her went much like the talks with the other folks. I learned later she had been crippled by tuberculosis that had moved into her spine.

"There's no way she could climb the hill to the mission even if we did have an elderly feeding program," I observed. "A lot of the people we've seen today would be in the same boat."

"Well, in that case, we'll have to figure out how to take meals to them," he replied, as we picked our way past open sewage ditches and through narrow alleys heading back toward the mission.

Larry's observation about the need for a *gran moun* feeding program was right on target. Now we just had to find a way to implement it.

When Dave and Vicki arrived two weeks later, we took them on a similar walk through the city, pointing out many of the same people Larry and I had seen earlier.

"We need to get this program up and running quickly," Vicki said urgently. "These people can't wait. So how do we finance it, Larry?"

"I think I know a way. Last time I was home, some folks at my church in Kentucky asked me what needs they could support. They gave me some seed money to use as God leads. I know this project would appeal to them. Would you like to put together a proposal?"

"Absolutely," Dave responded. "I'm really excited to be able to get busy meeting such a crucial need. Tell me, what facilities and equipment do you think we'd have to put in place?"

Within the next month, Dave found space in an empty area behind the birthing center that Magdala had recently opened. He hired two Haitian ladies to do the cooking, and with the help of an interpreter, Vicki interviewed about a dozen elderly folks who could walk up the steep path to the mission each afternoon for a meal of rice and beans.

On the first day I wanted to be there to see the program in action. Even though the people were supposed to come at 4:00, by 3:30 about eight of them had arrived.

"The food isn't ready," Vicki said. "What will we do with them until then?"

I began singing one of the Haitian hymns that I'd learned and was quickly joined by several enthusiastic voices. When we finished, a bright-eyed little old lady wearing a flowered straw hat stood up and led another song. Pretty soon everyone was clapping and smiling as they sang about *Jezi*.

I wish people in the States would sing with this much spirit, I thought.

Folks in Haiti really love to sing about *Jezi*.

Soon Vicki indicated that the food was ready. I asked the people to bow their heads, and I prayed for the health of these people, for the mission, and I thanked the Lord for this nutritious food. Everyone added a heartfelt "Amen, amen," and Dave, Vicki and I distributed their bowls of rice and beans.

"*Mèsi anpil*," each one said with a big smile as they began eating hungrily.

"How are we going to get food down to that little lady who can't walk?" I asked after everyone had been served.

"Just this morning a young teenager came into the courtyard asking if we had any work for him," Dave said. "His father hurt his back building the birthing center and has been unable to work ever since. Let's hire the boy to deliver meals to those who can't walk this far."

"That's a great idea," Vicki said. "We could buy some of those stacked dishes that we saw at the market last Saturday, fill them with food, and have him take it down to them. They could empty the food into their own bowls so that he could bring the dishes back up here to be used again."

"I think that'll work. Can you find him again to see when he could start?" I asked.

"As a matter of fact, he's still hanging around hoping that we'll offer him a job. I'll go get him."

Pretty soon Dave returned with a boy of about fourteen who smiled at us when he was introduced as Samuel. I recognized him from church. When I reached out to shake his hand, he politely greeted me with, "*Bonswa, Mis Pat. Koman ou ye?*"

We learned that he had five brothers and sisters, and that his family of eight lived in just one room.

"Since my father got hurt, it is very hard for my mother to take care of us all. I need to earn some money to help my family."

"I think we have a job for you," Dave said. He explained the need to deliver meals to the *gran moun* downtown, and the two of them agreed that he would start on Monday.

"*Mèsi anpil,*" Samuel said gratefully, "and *mèsi Jezi!*"

As he left to tell his family the good news, the elderly folks were also getting ready to leave. Several of them gave us hugs and toothless smiles, murmuring "*Bondye beni ou*" (God bless you) in our ears as they headed out the mission gate.

Vicki turned to me as the Haitian ladies in the kitchen started cleaning up the huge cast aluminum cooking pots, scraping the stuck-on rice into a slop bucket for the pigs.

"Aren't these *gran moun* delightful?" she exclaimed. "Now I know why you love the Haitian people. I'm so glad that Dave and I decided to come to the mission. I think this program is off to a good start, and I can hardly wait to reach the folks downtown. But I've definitely got to learn more Creole so that I can converse with them."

"We'll practice some common phrases tonight after dinner," I assured her. "It won't be long before you pick up the language if you listen and keep trying to use it."

CHAPTER FOURTEEN

When I first arrived at the mission in 1989, only two or three groups of short-term mission workers would come in each year, primarily to help with construction projects. These teams were from Kentucky where Larry had the most connections. The longer I stayed, the more I realized that if we had broader support from the States, we could accomplish more of God's work. Since it was nearly time for me to go on my first furlough, I intended to share our mission's vision and work with my home church in Illinois. I also needed to earn some money to meet my own personal expenses in Haiti.

One day I walked around the mission campus taking pictures of activities that would interest people back home. I planned to have slides made to use during my talks since pictures convey so much more than mere words.

People always enjoy seeing little kids, I figured, so I started with the children's feeding program. I began by asking Anamarie, one of our cooks, if I could take her picture. She was a delightful and hard-working lady with a happy disposition. As she dished up the children's breakfast of spaghetti noodles, I snapped her picture. I moved over to the tables where the children were eating and took a group shot. Navius was still living with me, so I asked him to smile for the camera. I wanted to share my Haitian "son" with the folks in Illinois.

My next stop was the new birthing center. Even though it was beastly hot in the room, giving birth here was far safer for mother and child than in a hut up in the hills. Two young women were in labor when I arrived. Magdala and another midwife were attending to the ladies, reminding them to breathe deeply, and checking their progress. One was enduring her pains quietly, but the other cried out as the baby began to come.

"Push hard," Magdala said to the young girl of no more than sixteen. "Now once more. That's right. Here comes your baby. We need another push."

Soon I heard the wail of the baby as Magdala held up a little boy for the mother to see. What a wonderful picture of the midwife and the new baby I would have to show at my home church!

I waited while Magdala cut the cord. The other midwife washed and dressed the baby and gave the tiny infant to the new mother. For a Haitian newborn he was a good size, about five pounds. I asked the new mother if I could take a picture. She nodded and smiled tiredly.

As I left, the second woman began moaning, and I knew that soon there would be another little one coming into the world.

Since it was only 2:00 p.m. and the elderly folks wouldn't arrive for awhile, I decided to capture some street scenes. Outside the gate a woman had spread out colorful dresses and shoes on the ground that she hoped to sell.

"Photo?" I asked, and she nodded.

As I stood at the top of the hill looking down on the city, I noticed what looked like cookies laid out neatly on a nearby rooftop. I walked toward the house where a woman was climbing down some crude stairs with two flimsy trays.

"*Bonjou, madanm,* what are you carrying?" I asked.

"These are *biskwit* which I make to sell."

I had heard about such "cookies" before, but hadn't seen them in this region. When the price of rice gets too high, people make mud pie biscuits out of dirt, cooking oil, and salt and lay them out to bake in the sun. It's the only "food" some people can afford to relieve their hunger.

"May I take your picture?"

"*Wi*," she said as she straightened her dress and held out the flat basket of "cookies."

This picture really will be worth a thousand words, I thought.

A little further down the road another woman was cooking what looked like a stew in a large iron pot over a charcoal fire. As a man stopped to buy what was probably his only meal of the day, they also agreed to let me take their picture.

I hoped to get a good photo of a Haitian woman carrying a heavy burden on her head. Sure enough, before long I was rewarded by two women approaching me, balancing cumbersome loads that they steadied with one hand. They both nodded agreeably when I raised my camera into view. As I snapped the picture, I noted that one had a tub full of clothing, and the other was carrying coconuts. Again I was struck by how strong their necks must be to support such weight.

Soon a young boy came along leading a donkey loaded down with saplings that would likely serve to repair a house. I asked for his picture, but he shook his head and put up his hand. A little puzzled by his reaction, I honored his refusal and hoped another donkey would come along soon.

By this time, I saw the first of the *gran moun* slowly making her way towards the mission gate. She saw my camera, stopped, and gave me a big smile. Before she moved on, she came closer and hugged me warmly.

"*Grangou?*" I asked.

"*Wi,*" she answered rubbing her stomach. "*Mèsi anpil,*" she said, pointing to the building where she would get her meal.

I walked in with her and took a few pictures as the cooks filled the bowls and Dave and Vicki served the folks.

When Samuel arrived, the cooks filled three stacked dishes for the handicapped folks downtown. While he waited, I asked him why some people objected to having their picture taken and others didn't mind.

"It has to do with voodoo," he said. "They think a photo steals their soul. But it's fine with me if you take my picture." He posed proudly as he headed for the mission gate with his load of "meals on feet."

I would be traveling back to the States for my month off with a group of twenty who had come for two weeks from Lexington, Kentucky. Since it was June, the group included several teenagers.

Two of the high school girls approached me in the courtyard as I left the *gran moun* feeding program. They wondered if they could see a baby being born. I didn't know how a woman giving birth would feel about having an audience, but I introduced them to Magdala who asked permission from the mother currently in labor. She surprised us by agreeing to have the girls stay. Magdala said that could pray for her and wipe her brow.

At dinnertime I asked the girls if the baby had come yet.

"Oh, yes, and I got to hold her!" said Jenny.

"The mom asked if we would pick out a name since she already had eight children and had run out of ideas. We thought and thought and finally decided on Angel because that's what she looked like to us!" Maria said excitedly.

Each evening we had devotions and sharing time. Once again my camera was busy, and I could see my program developing. Surely a few from my home church might be inspired to support the mission or even send a team of their own another year.

On the final night, Larry asked people where they had seen Jesus during their stay. Surprisingly, every single person was willing to get up and share a personal experience. I was particularly moved by Jenny's story.

"Maria and I watched two healthy babies come into this world a couple of days ago. One mom asked us to name her little girl since it was her ninth child. We named her Angel and prayed over her that God would take care of her, despite her being the youngest in such a large family.

"So today I decided to go back to the birthing center, but today's birth wasn't such a happy one."

She choked up, and it took a minute or two before she could continue.

"The mom was only eighteen and was so scared. The baby was delivered breech. When Magdala finally got her out, she didn't cry, and we realized that she was stillborn. I didn't know how to help the young mother. She's just a year older than I am and had to go through a hard pregnancy only to give birth to a dead baby."

By this time, Jenny was sobbing and I went up and put my arm around her.

Such outcomes are all too common in Haiti, I thought, but to Jenny it was an unexpected and devastating experience. It was time to turn to God.

"Dear God, we come to you tonight with heavy hearts. We ask you to comfort the young woman who lost her baby today. Even though we grieve, we give thanks that the baby is at home with you and did not have to suffer the hardships of hunger and poverty.

"We also pray for Jenny who witnessed this tragic outcome on her last day here. Help her remember the positive experiences as well as what happened today. We pray for safe travel for all of us tomorrow as we return to our homes. Help us to share our stories. May others be moved by what has meant so much to us. In Jesus' name. Amen."

After devotions I suggested that Jenny return to the birthing center with me. I thought it might help her to pray with the young woman. When we entered the room where the woman was resting, Jenny hugged her, and we took her hands in ours.

"Jenny, would you like to pray for our friend?" I asked, offering to translate.

She nodded and bowed her head, gathering her thoughts. After a few seconds, she began to speak.

"Loving Father, we come to you tonight on behalf of Celina who needs you. Wrap your arms around her, Lord. I pray that she will come to know you and that you will heal her heart and spirit. We know that her baby is already in heaven where you are taking care of her. May your presence give Celina comfort. We pray in Jesus' name. Amen."

Celina squeezed our hands, whispering a soft *mèsi* as we said our good-byes. The next day she would make the sorrowful journey back to her hut in the hills to bury her baby. Yet I was thankful she had come to the mission to give birth. I knew that all too often, both mother and child are lost when there are complications far from medical help.

As we went back upstairs, Jenny thanked me for suggesting that we visit Celina again.

"I think praying together helped both her and me, and I feel much better than earlier," she said. "Maybe I'll be able to sleep tonight after all."

Suddenly that night in Marchand Dessalines when God spoke to me about sharing the Good News in Haiti came back to me.

"You know, Jenny, God has shown me that Americans can't effectively preach to Haitians who don't already know Jesus. But we can minister to them as you did tonight. Celina will tell her friends how you prayed for her in God's name. Maybe as a result she'll want to learn about Jesus."

Jenny gave me a quick hug and we headed for bed. It would be a short night.

"Thank you, Lord, for helping me minister to Jenny. I'm sure your healing power was at work today."

CHAPTER FIFTEEN

"Mama Pat, do you really have to go home?" Navius asked. "Can't I go with you? Who will take care of me while you're gone?"

My five year old "adopted son" clung to me as I prepared to leave for the summer with the Kentucky group. Both of us were crying as I handed him over to Vicki.

"Sometime I'll take you to the States with me, but I can't this time, honey," I said. "Vicki will take good care of you while I'm away, and the next thing you know, I'll be back."

I had considered taking him home with me but wanted to talk with my family about their little "brother" before introducing him in person. Since I needed money, I planned to stay through September and hoped that I could work at the nursing home for several weeks. Since I also planned to travel to different parts of Illinois on this visit, such activities would be hard if I had Navius with me. One of my goals was to share about the mission as often as churches would invite me.

Reluctantly, he went to Vicki and waved goodbye. I climbed on the back of the truck to go downtown where we'd catch a bus for the long hot ride to Port-au-Prince.

I stayed in southern Illinois for three months, spending time with my children and Enid and speaking at several churches including my own. I was pleased when Pastor Bill said he'd like to lead a group to our mission the following summer.

"The pictures of programs at your mission really moved me," he said. "I think some of our teachers and teens would be interested during summer vacation. Would July be a good time for us? Do you have other groups then?"

"No, medical teams come in January and June, but we're definitely interested in hosting more church groups. Hopefully, you could bring some men to work on construction projects since we have plans to expand. We can always use nurses to help in the clinic as well."

"Oh, I know just the person for that if she can get time off from her job. I assume we'd have to raise our own money for transportation and expenses, wouldn't we?"

"Yes, but often friends and family will contribute to this kind of trip. At least that's how the folks from Lexington do it. They've been overwhelmed at how generous people are for this cause."

Just as promised, Miss Spence at the nursing home welcomed me with open arms when I approached her about working during my furlough.

"One of our practical nurses just had a baby, and I've been struggling to find someone to replace her," she said. "If you could fill in for the three months she's out with her baby, that would help us all out."

I began work the next day. It was easy to get back into the routine.

"How I've missed your visits with me, Pat! No one sits and talks with me the way you used to after you finished your shift," said Adeline when I brought her pills and took her blood pressure. "Come here and give me a hug."

As I hugged her, I felt sorry that she had no one to visit her. Maybe I could talk with Pastor Bill to see if someone in our church could stop by on a regular basis. I wondered how many other residents felt the same loneliness.

As usual I was staying with Susan and Jerry. He had already sold the cows, and I was eager to hear where they were on their future plans. One evening the three of us were enjoying sitting on the front porch after the kids went to bed.

"Now that you've sold the cows, what's your next step?" I asked.

This time it was Susan who volunteered the information.

"Jerry will be starting his classes at Bible College in September. Did Miss Spence tell you that I'll be working in the office at Lutheran Care Center? She says that I can work three days a week, and Connie has agreed to take care of Ruthie and Johnny on those days. Since Ruthie goes to kindergarten in the mornings, it's perfect that she can get off the bus at noon at Connie's."

"This is a major change for everyone, isn't it?" I remarked.

"Yes, when Jerry first mentioned his dream, I could only see the negatives. I didn't want to leave the kids, I knew we'd have to be much more frugal with our money, and we wouldn't have much time together. I guess I really threw a 'wet blanket' on his idea for awhile."

Jerry nodded with a twinkle in his eye.

"You certainly did," he said. "But God works in mysterious ways. Susan was impressed with my sermon during our pastor's vacation, but even that didn't convince her."

"I told him that there was more to being a minister than just preaching, which he already knew. However, I realized several weeks ago when we were having a congregational meeting that he has some real pastoring skills. An outside youth organization had asked to use our building for a coffee house several evenings a week.

"Our congregation was terribly divided about it. Some people worried about the building being misused while others thought it was a good way to serve the community. People were interrupting and shouting at each other. Our pastor had completely lost control. It was horrible for Christians to be acting that way toward each other.

"When Jerry got up to speak, I grabbed at his jacket to try to stop him, but he brushed my hand away."

Tears filled her eyes, and I could imagine how tense the situation had been.

"I wasn't sure I could calm people down, but God gave me the words to say in favor of the program," Jerry shared. "Somehow what I said helped tempers cool. The coffee house will open right after the beginning of school. Fortunately, the leader who approached us is really good with young people, and our members are feeling much more positive."

"How did that meeting convince you to support his dream?" I asked, turning to Susan.

"It seemed like God kept giving him signs leading in that direction. Once he began to tell people how he felt called to the ministry, the church agreed to pay part of his tuition, and that clinched it for me." She smiled, looking at her husband affectionately.

"It won't be easy for any of us," Jerry said, "but I'm glad she's behind me now."

"Let's pray," I said, reaching for their hands.

"Dear Lord, Jerry and Susan have made a decision to serve you in a new way. The path won't be easy, and three or four years in seminary will seem like a long time. Be with them and give them strength when the going gets tough. We know that you're pointing Jerry in this direction. Help them to see beyond temporary obstacles to the long-term goal. In Jesus' name. Amen."

I squeezed their hands as we let go and looked up at each other.

"Thanks, Mom, you're such an inspiration to all of us," Susan said.

"Let me fill everyone's coffee cups," I said, standing to go inside. "I also have some things on my mind that I'd like to run by you."

When I returned, I told them about Navius and how I had taken him in.

"Hopefully there will be times when he'll come home with me, and I want to be sure he'll get a warm welcome. Do you think anyone will have trouble with my bringing a little Haitian child into our family circle?"

They exchanged a glance, and Jerry immediately answered.

"We wouldn't be very Christian if we did, now would we? I think it's wonderful that you're acting as his mother."

"How old did you say he is, Mom?" Susan asked. "Does he understand English?"

When I said that he was nearly five and was learning some English, she said, "He'll be just at the right age to play with our kids."

Now that I'd seen Susan and Jerry's positive reaction, I was eager to tell the rest of the family about Navius. It was as if Susan had read my mind.

"I think it's about time to invite everyone for a family gathering," Susan declared. "You've visited with us all individually since you came home, but it's been ages since we've had a family dinner. I think I'll call to see if everyone can come Sunday night. Is that okay with you, Mom?"

"Sounds good to me. I always like to see my kids and grandkids."

CHAPTER SIXTEEN

After spending the summer at home, I was eager to return to Haiti. I missed Navius and the other children who came to the clinic and the feeding program.

I had shown my pictures at several churches where I had connections. At the end of my presentation at my home church, a good friend came up to me and said, "Pat, I've just inherited several thousand dollars from my aunt who had no children. I think she would be really pleased if I gave you five thousand dollars to take to the children in Haiti."

It never ceased to amaze me how generous people were when they heard the story of the needs in Haiti. I hugged her and replied, "Sadie, you have no idea how much this means to me. I'll be able to fill a suitcase with children's Tylenol, cough syrup, and cold medicines that will be just what we need to stock the clinic. The rest of your gift can go for the feeding program. Thank you so much!"

"Receiving this money was totally unexpected for me, and I really wasn't sure how to use it. Your talk felt like God urging me to respond in honor of my aunt. I'd love to go with you when you shop for the medicines."

We agreed on a date for a shopping spree and lunch. The following Saturday, while enjoying our salads and coffee, Sadie asked me many questions about my life in Haiti.

"Is it hard to give up the things we take for granted here in the States? I can't imagine having to eat rice and beans daily or taking cold showers. And the heat and humidity that you described when you showed us the pictures must be unbearable. I don't think I could take it!"

I laughed.

"Sadie, didn't you grow up in the country and use an outdoor toilet when you were young? Did you have air conditioning in your farmhouse? Until you got spoiled with all the amenities we have now, you probably never gave a thought to your lifestyle."

She was quiet as she thought about her early years.

"I hadn't thought of it like that," she conceded.

"It does get hot," I admitted, "but there's usually a breeze off the ocean, especially at night. I like to sleep outside on the roof under more stars than you've ever seen. Our skies here aren't that bright because of the streetlights, but there's a real sense of God's presence when I'm looking up at the night sky and praying before I go to sleep. I imagine it's how David felt as a young shepherd when he wrote so many of his psalms."

Sadie squeezed my hand and smiled.

"Pat, you're something else. You really inspire me. Perhaps I can visit the mission one summer with a team from our church."

"It would be wonderful to share with you firsthand what life is like down there," I said as we paid our bill and left the restaurant.

A week later I was on the plane descending into Port-au-Prince once again. I could hardly wait to be back home in St. Louis du Nord. As I went down the stairs from the plane, I was met by a wave of heat from the concrete below, and I recalled my conversation with Sadie. I wondered whether she could make the adjustment if she did come to visit the mission. This trip is not for everyone, I thought.

While I stood in line to go through customs, I noticed a couple wearing tee shirts with the name of the mission and its logo of three crosses on a map of Haiti. This year's shirt was bright green and very visible in a crowd.

I waited until they cleared customs and introduced myself.

"Hi, I'm Pat Hamilton," I said. "Welcome to Haiti. I see by your tee shirts that we're heading for the same place. I'm a missionary at the Northwest Haiti Christian Mission."

"I'm Bob Hastings, and this is my wife Sarah," he said, shaking my hand. "Our daughter came on a mission trip last summer, and her enthusiasm sparked a desire in us to serve. She told us about you, Miss Pat, but we didn't expect to be traveling to the mission with you. Are we ever glad to see you! We were a little anxious about this leg of the trip."

I tried to prepare them for the bus ride and suggested that we sit near the front if possible. They were real troopers and traveled very well. Still, viewing hour after hour of unspeakable poverty along just one road in Haiti was sobering for them. We stopped outside Gonaïves where everyone took a rest stop out in the bushes with the men in one area and the women in another.

"Well, that was a new experience," Sarah said bravely. "I'm glad I brought some tissues in my fanny pack."

"I hate to say it, but the roads get even worse from here to St. Louis," I told them as we made our way back to the bus.

"I hope you remembered to take some Dramamine before we started."

"I did, but I think I'll take another. I don't usually get motion sickness, but it might help me get some sleep on the rest of the trip."

I can sleep most anywhere, but not on the bus, I thought. With all the zig-zagging and honking, our seat cushions bouncing up and down from the bone-jarring bumps, and the choking dust and heat, it's really hard to sleep. But I chose not to say anything.

We had been on the road for another three hours when we came to the Big River near Port-de-Paix. I'd heard some of the Haitians saying that they had had several days of rain, and I wondered if we'd be able to cross. Sure enough, the river was very high and overflowing its banks.

"What happens now?" Sarah asked a little fretfully as the bus pulled to a stop on the muddy bank.

"Haitian drivers are really skillful, but if our driver decides it's too dangerous, we may have to cross by boat. Then hopefully, without the weight of passengers, the bus will be able to clear the high water."

Nearly at the end of her rope and on the verge of tears, Sarah laid her head dejectedly on Bob's shoulder.

"Oh, Bob, why did we ever decide to come down here? I wanted to serve God, but I didn't expect it to be like this," she cried.

"Let's get off the bus and pray," I suggested, and the rest of the passengers followed suit.

I led my new friends away from the crowded area and found a fallen tree where we sat down.

"Lord, seeing so much hardship for the first time is physically and emotionally draining. You've led your servants, Bob and

Sarah, to come here to Haiti, and now we've hit a roadblock. We ask for your help in crossing the river and that you will give us strength. In Christ's name I pray. Amen."

I squeezed their hands and looked up just in time to see a big empty dump truck arrive at the river's edge. Had God answered our prayer that quickly? I wondered, noticing the height of the truck and its large dual tires.

I could hear our bus driver talking with the truck driver. Soon he motioned to us to unload our bags and transfer them to the truck. God had heard our prayer, I realized, as I gathered my skirt, climbed onto the back bumper of the truck, and squeezed in between some Haitians to sit down on my suitcase. The empty bus was able to follow us, despite the fact that the water reached well above the tops of the tires. Soon we were back on the bus and headed toward Port-de-Paix and St. Louis.

Sarah seemed calmer now and began watching the sights as we bumped along. There was more vegetation in the Northwest, and we drove in and out of patches of shade. Some of the streets in Port-de-Paix were paved and smoother until we headed toward La Pointe. Since it was market day, we had to dodge the crowds of people buying and selling clothing, food, water, and vegetables. Soon we passed the old boatyard with its abandoned rusted ship aground just off shore. In La Pointe I pointed out the hospital where we occasionally send patients. Before long, I could see the welcoming sign on the arched entrance to St. Louis. On the left between the road and the ocean, we glimpsed the large cemetery with its ornate aboveground tombs behind a high blue wall. I felt my excitement rising, knowing that I was nearly home.

Once again we changed vehicles in order to travel up the steep pitted hill leading to the mission.

"You're finally here," I said to Sarah and Bob. I saw relief and renewed peace and confidence on their faces as the gate into the mission swung open.

"Welcome to the Northwest Haiti Christian Mission, your home for a month."

CHAPTER SEVENTEEN

As Bob, Sarah, and I jumped off the tap-tap, I heard an excited voice calling "Mama Pat, Mama Pat!" I looked up to the second floor where my Navius was waving madly. Soon he was running down the steps and into my arms.

"My, how you've grown! I can hardly lift you," I said, giving him a huge hug. Then I turned to Bob and Sarah and introduced my young charge.

Bob reached over and shook Navius' hand, and Sarah enveloped Navius and me in her arms.

"Have you adopted him?" she asked.

"Not officially, but in my heart, he's mine. I'll tell you more of his story later."

We headed across the courtyard to go upstairs. It seemed that every time I returned, our campus looked different because our programs were expanding so rapidly. We now had separate facilities for a clinic and a two-bed birthing center. And I noticed foundations for additional rooms that hadn't been there when I left a month ago.

"Navius, you've gotten so big that you'll have to get down. I can't carry you anymore," I said, setting him down and reaching for his hand. "I brought you a present. You can open it when we get upstairs."

His eyes sparkled as he tightened his grip and we went up to the open air dining area.

"What did you bring me? Can I see it now?" he asked excitedly.

"Hold on a second," I said as I saw Magdala approaching.

When we had embraced, I introduced her to Sarah and Bob, and she took them under her wing and showed them around so Navius and I could have our reunion.

"Oh, you brought me books. Can we read them now?" he asked impatiently as we went into my room.

"You can look at the pictures, and we'll read them together after we eat. I'm glad you like your books."

He lay down on my bed while I unpacked. It's so good to see him again, I thought as I put my things away. I've missed him so much.

Several days later I was working in the nutrition program when Lydie, one of the mothers, said to me, "Miss Pat, I would like to go to church on Sundays, but I can't go to the church downtown since I don't have good shoes or a nice dress like the other women."

It is true that most Haitian Christians get very dressed up when they go to church. I've often wondered how they can afford such beautiful outfits when many don't have enough money for food or rent. The men all wear dress shirts and ties, suits if they are leading the services, and little girls are decked out in frilly dresses, lacy socks, and ribbons in their tightly braided hair.

"God doesn't care how you dress to worship him, Lydie," I said. "He just wants you to praise him and pray and hear the Word about Jesus."

"Yes, I know God doesn't care, but other people do," she replied adamantly. "I just wouldn't feel right in my everyday work dress and worn-out shoes. People would look down on me."

An idea was forming in my mind to address the concerns of people like Lydie. I decided I'd talk with Larry to see if the mission could build a *choukoun* that would provide a more informal setting for worship. That evening at dinner I shared Lydie's dilemma with Larry.

"I can't tell you how many times I've heard that excuse," he said, "but I know it's true. I keep reminding them that people came to Jesus barefoot with only the clothes on their backs, but I can't convince them. Haitians dress better than the American groups who come here and worship with them.

"A *choukoun* wouldn't cost much," he thought aloud, "and we do have a group arriving in a couple of weeks. There's room for a small building like that right here in the courtyard. All we'd need is a circular pad of concrete with walls about two feet high and posts every ten feet or so to support a tin roof. It wouldn't take long to build because the sides would be left open."

"And we could use it during the week for the nutrition program," I said, getting excited. "It would provide shade for the moms and children."

Larry put his hand on his chin, something he often does when he's thinking.

"This will be a great way to reach more people with the Word! We'll have to find a preacher, but Dave and I can cover it until we can find a Haitian pastor. When the Americans are here, we'd need an interpreter."

"And Jude could handle the translating," I suggested.

If Larry gets enthusiastic about a project, it happens in a hurry. The Lexington group arrived two weeks later. It included three men who worked with several Haitians, and in less than a week, we were able to hold a church service.

We expected eight to ten people and were gratified to have twenty moms and children and some fathers show up, plus a couple of *gran moun*. Our service was a little disjointed since it was our first attempt, but when Jude led them in singing, their voices were loud and enthusiastic. By the time they began their third song, people were clapping, raising their hands in praise, and swaying to the music. A little boy with Down's syndrome was even dancing.

> Dave's message was based on Matthew 28:18-20.
> "Jesus came to them and said, 'All authority in heaven and on earth has been given to me. Therefore, go and make disciples of all the nations, baptizing them in the name of the Father and the Son and the Holy Spirit and teaching them to obey everything I have commanded you. And surely I will be with you always, to the very end of the age.' "

After Jude read the scripture in Creole, Dave began his sermon.

"I know that God is happy in heaven this morning! Nothing pleases him more than to see his children gathered together to worship him and sing his praises. The Bible says, 'Make a joyful noise' and you have done that this morning!"

As Jude translated each sentence, the people nodded enthusiastically. "Amen! Amen! Amen!" they shouted.

"Jesus was more than just a good man," Dave continued. "He was the son of the creator of the whole universe. Jesus' obedience to his father gave him power. 'All authority in heaven and on earth has been given to me.' It is right to come to church on Sunday to learn about and worship such a powerful God! It doesn't matter what we wear or how we look—God wants the best our hearts can offer.

"Because of his authority, Jesus has the right to instruct us. He said, 'Go and make disciples of all nations.' That's one reason we *blancs* have come to Haiti, because Jesus said we should. But his command isn't just for Mr. Larry, or Miss Pat, or me. His words are for you just as surely as they are for us. 'Go and make disciples.' You must talk to your friends and neighbors, to your children and family members, for Jesus wants *all* to be his disciples.

"Some of you may be believers but haven't been baptized. The Bible says, 'Repent and be baptized.' In a few weeks we will meet at the Big River where we'll follow Jesus' command to baptize his followers. If you want to accept Jesus and be baptized, please come forward as we pray."

Congregational prayer in Haiti is more intense and personal than in most American churches. As Dave started to pray for the future of the new church and for new believers to accept Christ, the swell of individual fervent voices drowned out his words. As always, it moved me deeply.

After the service, Lydie caught up with me while Larry and Dave talked with two people who had accepted Jesus that day.

"Thank you for helping start this church, Miss Pat. I am so happy that I can come here and sing and pray, and my children and I can learn about Jesus. *Mèsi Bondye!*"

On a breezy sunshiny day several Sundays later, the mission truck waited at the gate as people climbed in for the ride to the Big River. A small group of Americans was with us, and we all crowded in until the wooden planks along the sides of the truck were filled, as well as the bed of the truck.

As we started down the hill, Jude began singing "Amazing Grace" in Creole, and the Americans joined in English. Folks along the road looked at us curiously as we passed. Soon Jude chose a more upbeat song, and we all began clapping to the music. What a joy to be praising God as we bounced along the crowded road!

When we arrived, we climbed down alongside the busy riverbank. People who were doing laundry or bathing looked up when they heard us singing.

For the baptism Dave had chosen a scripture from Acts 2, which held a powerful promise. He began with Peter's words:

> "Repent and be baptized, every one of you, in the name of Jesus Christ, so that your sins may be forgiven.
> And you will receive the gift of the Holy Spirit."

Dave then beckoned to Lydie who came forward, her face shining with anticipation. The two of them waded into the river, Lydie pinched her nose, and Dave immersed her entire body in the water. When he lifted her out of the water, he proclaimed in a loud voice, "Lydie, I baptize you in the name of the Father, the Son, and the Holy Spirit. Your sins are forgiven."

She returned to her friends who reached for her hands, squeezed them as a sign of blessing, and wrapped her in a white towel. *"Mwen renmen Jezi!,"* (I love Jesus!) she exclaimed as she looked up to the heavens.

One by one, the others who were waiting their turn to be baptized joined Dave and an elder in the river. In all about ten Haitians and two Americans were baptized that day.

As we pulled ourselves up into the back of the truck, Jude broke into song again, and soon all of us were singing both in English and Creole.

"Alelou, alelou, alelou, alelouya, glwa o Segnè"

God delights in hearing his children singing his praises in any language, I thought. Putting my arm affectionately around Lydie's shoulder, I said, *"Bondye beni ou, zanmi mwen."* (God bless you, my friend.)

Only a few weeks after her baptism, Lydie approached me with another concern that was very important to her.

"You know, Miss Pat, I wish that my children and I could read the Bible for ourselves. That way we could learn more of God's Word. But I can't afford to send Pierre and Sabine to school where they could learn to read. You talked Mr. Larry into building us a church. Do you think you could ask him to start a school at the mission?"

Once again her comments made me think. The needs here in St. Louis never seem to end, I mused. Lydie is right in wanting her children to be able to read. There must be dozens of other mothers who desire the same thing for their children.

When I found a chance to broach the subject of a mission school with Larry, he was hesitant at first.

"What you are suggesting is an enormous commitment," he cautioned.

"Building and staffing a school is a much bigger undertaking than constructing a small *choukoun* church. But empowering people to read God's Word would be a huge blessing to them. Let's pray about it and see what God wants us to do."

This time we had to wait almost a year before God's plan for a school became clear.

"I've got a surprise for you," Larry said one day after the *gran moun* had finished their meal. "I'd like you to meet a good friend of mine, Pastor Ben from Indiana."

My hand nearly disappeared in the big man's firm grasp.

"Miss Pat, I'm delighted to meet you," he boomed. "I understand you've been praying fervently for funding to build a school here at the mission. Well, your prayers have been answered. A group from my church will be here next week to start construction out by the gate. The benefactor will be coming as well, but he doesn't want anyone to know the money is from him."

"That's wonderful!" I exclaimed. "I can hardly wait to share this news with Lydie. She has been so confident that God would provide this opportunity for her son and daughter."

As I lay down that night, I praised God for creating yet another opportunity for the mission to reach out. Little did I know that this would be the first of dozens of schools in the Northwest where hundreds of sponsored children would be educated through sixth grade. In no time at all, I fell asleep with a real sense of thankfulness in my heart.

CHAPTER EIGHTEEN

Within six months, we had outgrown the *choukoun* church. People were even sitting on mats on the ground outside during worship. It was clear we needed to find the money and manpower to build a more substantial structure.

Our prayers for funds were answered as a result of a sad situation. Larry shared with us news of the sudden death of a young American preacher who had brought a small group to Haiti.

"His church in Kentucky wants to do something meaningful in his memory. Since our mission was close to his heart, they want to contribute substantially to the construction of a larger church near the mission. So now we need to pray for land."

God works in mysterious ways, as we all know. Soon a neighbor whose brother owned property just outside the mission began coming to the *choukoun* church.

Not long after, Jude and I ran into him on market day as we threaded our way among the rickety stalls and noisy vendors. We told him how happy we were that he was coming to church.

"God is truly at work in St. Louis," Jude said. "Why, we only had a handful of people when we started the *choukoun* church, and now there's hardly room to turn around!"

"What you really need is a larger church," the man replied.

"We've been praying about that for some time," I responded, "but we have no place to build. It's in God's hands for now."

The next Sunday as the neighbor shook Larry's hand, I overheard him say, "If you are looking for land to build a bigger church, I think you should talk to my brother. Can you come with me to see some property that belongs to him? It's just down the street," he added.

They left right after church to meet the landowner. When Larry and Jude returned an hour later, we knew from their expressions that they had good news. With Jude's help, Larry had negotiated an agreement to buy the land. Soon we could break ground.

A team of nine men arrived in the middle of the next month from the sponsoring church in Kentucky. Before the end of their stay, they and several Haitian workers had erected a concrete block church on the site. They had to mix the cement for the floor in small batches at a time, using shovels to combine the piles of sand and dry concrete with water. The church was called *"Beni Bondye,"* which means "Bless God."

That first Sunday in the new church, the Kentucky team leader stood to address the congregation with tears in his eyes. "Our friend and pastor is looking down on us this morning from heaven, rejoicing that you have a place to worship and grow. We thank God for his life and the heart he had for his fellow Christians in Haiti."

What a blessing it was to have grown in just six months from the twenty people who began worshiping in the *choukoun* to the approximately eighty people who were now coming to church on Sundays. Although worshipers still tried to look their best, they now understood that they were there to praise and pray, and they knew that the Lord was pleased.

Within a couple of years as the "*Beni Bondye*" church began to burst its seams, it became clear that our Haitian brothers and sisters were indeed spreading the word about Jesus and inviting their friends to worship. The little church was overflowing with new believers. Every Sunday people crowded onto the benches, and many more had to stand during the services. Once more we began to pray that we'd find enough land for an even larger church so that the congregation could continue to grow.

It wasn't long before the mission was able to buy the land in front of the voodoo tree across the street. Little did we know how strongly the voodoo community would challenge our plans. This would lead to my first real experience of being persecuted for Christ. But our God is a faithful God, and he would provide us with the courage to stand firm on that fateful day when we'd find ourselves with snakes and nasty liquid hurled in our faces.

Building a larger church would require a major commitment of both money and workers. We again recognized God's response when a pastor and outreach committee in Cincinnati attended a Midwest mission conference.

"We've been supporting your mission for a number of years," the minister said to Larry after his presentation. "We feel led to offer our congregation the chance to become more deeply invested. What's your greatest need at present?"

The answer, a bigger church, was obvious. As soon as they could raise the funds, recruit volunteers, and finalize their plans, the first of several teams arrived with dedicated people eager to get started. The foundation had to be massive, as the back part of the church would extend at least two stories down the side of the hill. As construction progressed, I watched the hard work of dozens of men from St. Louis who could now provide for their families, thanks to this project. I thought what a blessing this church was even before it was completed.

Several folks from that Cincinnati church became "regulars" on summer mission trips. One day when we'd been in the new church for about two years a woman joined me at lunch. It was Rachel's first trip, and she was excited to be at the mission she'd heard so much about.

Looking across the courtyard, we could clearly see the top of the enormous white cross outlined against the breathtaking blue sky.

"The Citadel church is even bigger than I imagined," Rachel remarked. "And I could see that cross all the way from the square downtown when we first arrived!"

"Yes, the cross is your church's latest project. No doubt you've heard that erecting it was quite a feat," I added. "Would you like to see it up close tonight after dinner? You can see most of St. Louis from the roof, and there's a wonderful view of the ocean."

She loved the idea. At sunset we grabbed our flashlights and went across the road into the churchyard. I unlocked the gate to the tower, and we climbed the wrought-iron staircase to the roof.

"How beautiful," she gasped as we emerged into the vibrant display of pinks, purples, and oranges splashed across the sky. Together we gazed out over the ocean toward the island of Tortuga. We were silent for some time as the daylight gradually faded.

"This cross reminds the people of St. Louis du Nord of Christ's presence," I said to my companion. "It's visible for miles around. In fact, on the very first night that it was lit up, there was a terrible storm. An overcrowded sailboat from

Tortuga capsized far from shore, and everyone on board was in danger of drowning. Yet all forty people were able to swim to safety in the heavy seas. Each time they crested a wave, they could see that lighted cross guiding them to shore. That night people truly experienced the saving power of the cross."

We sat on a bench looking at the myriad of bright stars that had emerged in the heavens, listening to the waves lapping at the shore, and sensing the peace that comes from being in God's presence.

"Thank you, Miss Pat, for sharing the story of that miracle with me. I'm in awe that God used my church as part of his plan," she said as we felt our way down the spiral staircase.

CHAPTER NINETEEN

I really wanted to take Navius for his first visit to the States to meet my family, but I knew that getting him out of Haiti and into the U.S. would involve a lot of "red tape." After all, both his parents were dead. I decided that he and I should make a trip to Port-au-Prince to the American Embassy to find out what would be required. Since his aunt did have a birth certificate for him, I knew that would help. As his legal guardian, she gave me a letter saying that he could travel with me. The people at the Embassy had me sign a statement that I would be responsible for him in the U.S., and I paid $700 for his first passport.

In January, six months after going to the Embassy, I began to wonder if I'd ever hear back from the Embassy. It was an entire year after first applying for the passport before I finally had all the legal papers in hand. We made plans to leave in June when he would be finished with second grade at the English-language school in Port-de-Paix.

"You'll get to fly on a big airplane to Miami and then a second one to another St. Louis, this one in Missouri!" I told him.

His eyes got really big with excitement.

"You've told me all about your other children," he said. "Will they like me?"

"Come here," I said, patting my lap.

As he cuddled up to me, I put my arms around him and reassured him.

"We'll be staying with my daughter Susan who has two children close to your age. You'll enjoy playing with Ruthie and Johnny. We'll go to the zoo like the one in your book. And you'll get to see the Mississippi, the biggest river in America!" I told him.

He reached up and hugged me and asked if he could read the zoo book to me. As I listened I thought proudly what a good education he was getting. By this time he was speaking English well, and I felt that he'd make an easy adjustment to a vacation in the U.S.

After the long bus ride to the capital, we had some extra time at the airport in Port-au-Prince.

"Let's go look for some gifts from your country for you to take to Ruthie and Johnny. There are two or three nice shops upstairs," I said, taking his hand.

In the first shop he exclaimed, "Look at this tap-tap bus with holes in the top! I like how they painted it. But what are the holes for?"

"I think it's a pencil holder. Do you think that would be a good gift from Haiti?" I asked.

"Oh yes! See all the people inside? And I like the bright colors. Did you say that Ruthie goes to school? She could put her pencils in these holes."

"That's a good present for her. What do you see that you think Johnny would like? He's about four now."

"Look at this tap-tap truck," he said pointing to a colorful wooden toy. "And its wheels work! I think Johnny would like this one, don't you?" He smiled up at me.

"It's perfect, Navius, and I see just what to get for Susan and Jerry. I know they'll like that manger scene over there with the little clay figures that fit inside a coconut."

As I paid for our gifts, I glanced at my watch and realized that we needed to hurry downstairs since it was nearly time to board.

"Look, Navius, see the big airplane over there?" I pointed out as we exited the terminal. "That's what we're going to fly in. Won't that be fun?"

"Oh, Mama Pat, I'm scared. What makes it stay up in the sky?"

I shook my head. I really didn't have a good answer for that question.

"Just trust me that it's safe. God will take care of us on this trip," I said.

Twelve long hours later, after making it through customs, a layover, and changing planes, a very tired little boy was sound asleep in the seat next to me as our plane descended into St. Louis. I tapped him lightly on the arm.

"Wake up, Navius, we're starting to land, and soon you'll be seeing Ruthie and Johnny."

He yawned and stretched and then glued his face to the window.

I had to hang on tightly to his hand as we walked through the airport. He was fascinated with the moving sidewalks, the escalators, and the high-speed train that transported us from one concourse to another.

"So many moving things, Mama Pat. I didn't see all this in the airport in Haiti."

In the distance I could see people waiting, and soon I recognized my daughter and her family. I also could feel Navius pulling back behind me, probably feeling a little shy.

"Mom, it's good to see you. It's been so long this time," Susan said as she gave me a warm hug. "And this must be Navius!"

She knelt down and reached for his hand. Timidly, he put his hand in hers.

"Ruthie and Johnny, this is Navius, Grandma's little boy from Haiti. Can you shake hands with him? He's just about the same age as you, Ruthie."

Both of them stretched out their hands and shook his.

"Don't you have something to share?" Susan prompted.

They reached deep into their pockets. Ruthie handed Navius a grape lollipop, and Johnny gave him a bag of M&M's.

"*Mèsi*," he said softly.

Jerry smiled at me, knelt down to Navius's level, and helped him open the M&M's, which he promptly shared. As the kids munched on the chocolates, Jerry said, "Let's go find your luggage."

On our way to the parking garage, I offered a short prayer.

"Dear Lord, I hope I've done the right thing in bringing Navius to this country. It's hard to know what's best for him. Give me wisdom during this visit. And thank you for our safe travel. Amen."

CHAPTER TWENTY

The airport was just the beginning of exciting adventures for Navius. At the zoo he used my camera to take dozens of pictures of elephants, zebras, giraffes, kangaroos, and especially the monkeys. He was captivated watching them swing from tree to tree and hang by their tails.

Another day we rode the elevator to the top of the St. Louis Arch and looked out on the Mississippi River.

"That's even bigger than our 'Big River,'" he said. "but nobody's taking a bath or washing their clothes in it like back home."

Now that Cheryl was married and had a new house, she invited the entire family over for dinner one Sunday night. We all took some food to make it easier for her. Navius and I made cookies, and Susan and Jerry made homemade ice cream for dessert.

"One more thing that turns," Navius exclaimed, watching the electric ice cream maker.

When Jerry lifted the cover off, he let the kids lick the paddle.

"So good, Uncle Jerry," said Navius, wiping a sticky drip from his chin.

At Cheryl's house Navius met the rest of the family including Phil, Lynn's new husband. After dinner the kids went outside to play, and the adults gathered on the back porch.

Lynn had been rather quiet most of the evening, I'd noticed. Finally, she spoke up.

"Mom, Phil and I have been talking about how we'd like to see firsthand what you do in Haiti. We'd like to take time off from work and spend a few months down there. Since we're both nurses, we think we could be of use."

I had always hoped that someone from my family might be interested in visiting the mission.

"Now seems to be the right time for us to go before we start our family," Phil chimed in. "If that sounds good to you, I think we'd have time to let our bosses know that we'd like a leave of absence."

"Navius and I will be here for four more weeks," I said. "See what you can work out. A surgical team is scheduled for the end of next month, and I'm sure they'll be happy to have two nurses who can help with aftercare."

Early that August Lynn, Phil, Navius, and I flew out of the St. Louis airport headed for Haiti. When we arrived in Miami, Navius fell asleep in the airport, and I took the opportunity to fill the others in on the background of the new surgery program.

"This is quite a story," I began. "Back in February we were surprised when a surgical nurse named Corinne arrived unannounced at the mission. She had been working in Port-au-Prince, and she had rented a car to come north at the request of a friend who was sponsoring a child in our school. She drove by herself all the way up to St. Louis du Nord and stayed with us for a couple of weeks. She recognized that many people were being served at the clinic and birthing center, but she challenged us to do more.

"Corinne left instructions for us to prepare a room to be used for surgery and said that she'd be back in six months with a surgeon and some supplies and equipment. We expect that she and this Dr. Bush will be arriving next week. Magdala has been screening patients for surgery while the doctor and Corinne are with us. You both will be extremely valuable in prepping patients and in post-op. I should warn you, however, not to expect the set-up to be as sterile or efficient as you're used to."

"I hope we can adjust to working in such conditions," said Phil, looking a little uncertain as he glanced over at Lynn.

The flight to Port-au-Prince was smooth, and there were no mishaps during the grueling bus ride up to the mission. Having glimpsed the desperate poverty on the long bus trip, Phil and Lynn arrived motivated to begin their work.

On the day that Corinne and Dr. Bush were due to arrive, a man appeared, doubled over and in terrible pain.

"Looks like a gall bladder problem to me," Phil said, after a quick examination in the clinic. "I hope Dr. Bush gets here soon. This man is really miserable."

"While you're waiting, why don't you see what you can rig up for lighting in the surgery room?" I suggested. "The painting, tiling, and plumbing are done, but they'll need more direct light to be able to operate. Look around the compound to see what you can find to hang above the surgical table in there."

"Where would I find a bright light?" he asked.

"Try down by the garage where they work on the trucks. They might have a headlight down there which you could hook up so the doctor can see what he's doing."

Before long Phil returned triumphantly clutching a headlight that he managed to suspend above the table. Clearly, he was starting to see how to accomplish more with less.

"As long as the generator works, we'll be in business," I said. "God willing, it won't quit on us this next week or so."

The sound of a truck in the courtyard interrupted our conversation. We went outside just as Corinne and Dr. Bush were climbing down from the mission truck. I greeted Corinne with a big hug and the doctor with a warm handshake.

"Are you too exhausted to go right to work?" I asked them. "We have what appears to be a gall bladder patient in excruciating pain."

"Whew, I thought we'd have a few hours to catch our breath before starting in," Corinne replied, and the doctor nodded. "Do you have anything for us to eat first? We haven't eaten all day, and we really need to clean up."

After about an hour, Lynn and Phil joined them in the surgery room where Dr. Bush successfully performed the gall bladder surgery.

"It's a good thing you two got here when you did. Now, why don't you two get some rest and let Lynn and Phil look out for your patient?" I suggested.

The next week was filled with a variety of surgeries from removing growths to appendectomies to a bowel resection. Lynn and Phil stayed very busy with patient care. It was clear that God had inspired them to come at a time when they were badly needed.

The day after Corinne and Dr. Bush left, Lynn came to find me in my room before bedtime.

"Mom, we've seen so many elderly people in surgery this past week. Some of them seem totally neglected. We operated on a man yesterday whose leg needed to be amputated because of gangrene. He had fallen in the square, and the boys who take food downtown used a wheelbarrow to carry him all the way up here. But where was his family? Why didn't they get him help?"

"Come sit down on the bed with me, honey," I said, smoothing the spread.

"I'll bet many of the *gran moun* you've seen have outlived their children and are completely alone. Some of them are homeless, I'm sure."

"Can't the mission give them a home?" Lynn asked. "How can they survive?"

"I think you've pointed out something that hadn't been put into words before. We'll have to run it by Larry, of course, and resources are always an issue. But if it's God's will that we care for these elderly 'orphans,' then he'll show us the way."

Lynn nodded, taking my hand in hers and bowing her head to pray.

"Heavenly Father, Phil and I have been struck by the plight of the elderly here in St. Louis. Many of them are terribly at risk. They don't know about Jesus or your great love for them. We ask your guidance and direction in helping us find a way for them to live out their final years with dignity. In Jesus' name I pray. Amen."

"Oh Lynn, I'm so proud of you and Phil for leaving your jobs to come to Haiti and share in my ministry. I know that being here is not an easy adjustment, but it means more than I can tell you that you understand what keeps drawing me back. I can see that you really 'get it'. Let's hope that God will see fit to answer your prayers about a *gran moun* home."

She smiled at me affectionately and got up to go back to her room.

"Good night, Mom. Sleep well," she said as she closed the screen door behind her.

CHAPTER TWENTY-ONE

God never ceases to amaze me with his answers to our prayers. The land behind the mission became available, but we had to find the money to buy it. Several weeks later, Larry's wife Diana and their adult son Janeil spoke at another church in Cincinnati. They needed $10,000 to purchase the land on which to build a home for the elderly. Two days later a check for that exact amount arrived from a couple who had heard their appeal. Praise the Lord!

Over the course of the next year, as short-term teams and Haitians worked together, a hillside was excavated with shovels and wheelbarrows, and the foundation was laid. Within six months, the building had progressed to include three large rooms: a dorm room for the men, another for the women, and a central room in between. Out front was a long porch that reminded us of a popular chain of Southern-cooking restaurants back home.

"Wouldn't it be wonderful if we had enough rocking chairs for our residents to sit outside and rock?" Diana often commented.

Once again a church responded by donating a dozen rocking chairs that were shipped in with mattresses for the dorm rooms. Soon it was moving day for the fifteen or so *gran moun* we had identified as being homeless and having no relatives. Among them was Rosalinda. We had been taking her food every afternoon for several weeks before her daughter's death a month before. Now someone else occupied what had been their home, and Rosalinda was living in the alley nearby.

As Larry drove the mission's pickup truck downtown past the dilapidated closely spaced buildings, I thought back to a dozen years earlier when I had first arrived in St. Louis. In the early 1990's I could walk through these streets and see lots of open space. Now, crowded alleyways filled the area between the three main parallel roads, and roofless concrete block buildings with partial walls awaited the funds to complete another level. How the small city had mushroomed!

We started down by the waterfront where we had first seen Rosalinda lying on her mat. Larry stopped the truck, and we both went over to talk with her. Her clothes were tattered, her gray hair was matted, and her faded flip-flops did little to protect her cracked calloused feet. As we approached her, we could see that she was asleep.

"I don't want to startle her," I said quietly.

"She'll be okay," Larry said as he touched her arm.

Although she jumped at his touch, when she saw who we were, her wrinkled face broke into a smile.

"Did you come to get me?" she asked. "I've been waiting all day. See, I'm packed and ready to go!"

Larry picked up the half-filled pillowcase that contained all of Rosalinda's worldly possessions. I reached for her hand to steady her, and she stepped gratefully onto the stool we had brought, climbing slowly onto the tailgate and into the truck.

A similar scene was repeated in several places until there were seven of our homeless old folks perched in the truck.

Soon we were riding down the driveway behind the mission to the brand new *gran moun* home.

Maureen, our pharmacist, and two college interns who were with us that summer, greeted our future residents. They showed the new arrivals to the dorms where their beds were all made up, then to the common room where their afternoon meal was waiting. Lisa and Molly served up heaping bowls of rice and beans.

The mission had hired the mother of three young children to prepare the food. Her husband had no job, so what she earned as a cook was the family's only steady source of income.

"Mr. Larry, *mèsi anpil* for this wonderful home," Rosalinda said, giving him a big hug after she finished her meal.

"*Wi, mèsi, mèsi,*" echoed the rest of them. "Now we have a safe place to sleep!"

"Come outside and sit a spell," I invited them after they had eaten.

Soon all seven of them were rocking contentedly. Within a few minutes, several had dozed off as the excitement of the move and the comfort of a full stomach caught up with them.

"What a great day!" I declared. "I think we need to offer praise and thanksgiving."

We missionaries circled up in the common room and Larry began to pray.

"Heavenly Father, thank you for the opportunity to minister to these, your abandoned children. We are truly grateful for the generous people back in the States who have made this home possible. We ask that sponsors will be forthcoming to cover each resident's expenses so that we can continue the good work you've begun here. Please bless these people and help them come to know your Son as their Lord and Savior. We ask all this in Jesus' name. Amen."

We squeezed hands as Larry finished praying. Lisa and Molly planned to stick around the first night to help the new residents get settled.

The next afternoon we went the other direction where we made a second sweep to pick up several more people we knew needed a home. When we delivered them to the front porch, Rosalinda was the first one to welcome them home. I hardly recognized her with her hair cleaned and brushed and a different dress.

During the next week, we made it a point to see each of the *gran moun* in the clinic to assess their general health. Aside from being frail, they had remarkably few problems.

"I can't believe how resilient these people are," Maureen observed. "Considering the fact that life expectancy in Haiti is only around age fifty-five, the fact that they have survived living on the street is almost miraculous."

It wasn't long before most had regained their strength and were putting on some weight. In addition, they were enthusiastic attendees at Sunday services, so they were receiving spiritual sustenance as well.

"Isn't it encouraging to see what food, shelter and a good night's sleep will do to revive people?" I asked Maureen one Sunday after church.

She nodded. "It's good to be involved in sharing God's love in such a concrete way and to be so appreciated."

I had to agree with her. "Thank you, Lord," I prayed silently, "for leading me to serve in this corner of your world. Amen."

CHAPTER TWENTY-TWO

"Miss Pat, how long have you been a missionary in Haiti?" Lisa asked as we stood in line for breakfast one morning toward the end of her summer internship.

I had to stop and think about it.

"Well, I first went to Marchand Dessalines in 1983, so I guess it's been almost twenty years," I said. "I can't believe how fast the time has gone."

"You must have seen a lot of changes over the years," she said, "and you have so many responsibilities here now. Don't you ever get tired?"

Getting tired hadn't really entered my head because I always kept so busy. But I had to admit that life was more hectic and stressful now that so many groups were coming in. My ministry seemed to have shifted from an emphasis on Haitians' needs to hospitality for Americans. When short-term teams were here, I had to exchange their dollars for Haitian gourdes, attend to any intestinal issues they developed, answer their questions, and sometimes give tours of the ever-changing campus. This was all in addition to my daily duties with the nutrition programs. Lisa's question made me think about my age since I was now seventy-three. It also awakened a familiar sense of restlessness within me.

"Fortunately, I sleep very well, but I do tire more easily than I used to," I conceded.

I carried my plate of biscuits and peanut butter to a table and sat down with Larry, Maureen, and Lisa. Larry was talking with some men from his home church in Lexington.

I overheard one of them saying, "I understand that Janeil is looking to find some land farther west at the Baie des Moustiques. How's that working out?"

"Actually, he's been able to acquire four acres with the help of a church in Indiana, and we hope to start putting up a building out there soon. We've had a presence in that area for several years through mobile medical clinics, revivals at night, and occasional food distribution."

As Larry was talking, Janeil brought his breakfast over and joined us.

"I hear you're talking about the Baie," he said as he sat down. "A group of us are going out to the 'Far West' tomorrow to dedicate the land. Let me know if any of you would like to go along. We'll be leaving in the morning and will stay overnight."

Something stirred within me.

"What are your goals for starting a mission out there?" I asked, realizing that I might like to be a part of this new venture.

"Well, there's a fairly sizable but very poor community at the Baie and a small struggling church that we'd like to encourage. We'd start with a a clinic since there's no one out there with any medical training. How would you like to go see it?" he asked me.

"Count me in! I'd just need to find someone to cover for me here," I answered.

"We can make that happen," Janeil assured me.

His dad added, "Yeah, go ahead, Pat. You deserve a change of pace and a chance to relax. You've really been stretched thin here lately."

That night before bed, I gathered a bedroll and flashlight, packed my toiletries, and laid out a set of clean clothes plus my Bible. The next morning, about twenty of us piled into the bus. The back aisles and roof had been loaded with long wooden planks for revival seats, army surplus stretchers for us to sleep on, several big containers of drinking water, and a small generator with lights to string up for the service. Janeil estimated the trip would probably take at least two hours, depending on how easily we could get across the Big River in Port-de-Paix. Fortunately, it wasn't very high, and the bus made it through without any problems.

I knew from previous trips to the Baie that once we crossed the river heading west, the countryside would become much more arid and desert-like.

"I'm surprised to see so many kinds of cactus out here," one girl exclaimed. "I recognize organ pipe and saguaro and yucca plants!"

It was true, a wide variety of cacti grew alongside the road as far as the eye could see, with only an occasional scrawny tree or shrub offering any hope of shade.

"*Bonjou*" we'd call out every few minutes through the open windows when we'd encounter old ladies or young boys on donkeys. Usually they'd smile and wave back at us. Whereas in St. Louis it was common to see a few donkeys carrying their burdens, here we saw whole trains of heavily laden donkeys heading who knows where.

"Where do all these people live, and where are they going?" another of the group wondered aloud.

Hints of footpaths crisscrossed the landscape, but hardly any homes were visible from the road.

There's a whole different atmosphere out here, I thought. It's much more rural. I like it.

Soon the bus turned off the unpaved two-lane main road onto a narrower road with even deeper ruts. Clearly it had rained recently, and we all held our breath as one or two tires lost traction when the driver had to veer around big mud puddles.

After about twenty minutes on the narrower road, we passed a large rock quarry and caught our first glimpse of the ocean through an opening between the hills.

"I see the water!" a girl said excitedly. "Look how blue it is!"

Before long we came to a stop, and Janeil had us all get out. The land was flat and bare, pocked with sand crab holes and scraggly vegetation. It lay about a half mile from a beautiful curved sandy beach that was surrounded by a small village of thatched-roof huts. Roosters, goats, and pigs roamed freely between the houses. In the distance cows and sheep searched for any kind of foliage on the dusty rock-strewn mud flats. Big piles of branches smoldered under palm fronds where people were making charcoal to sell.

A few Haitians had come along with us to build benches for use during the dedication service. As they began their work, some of the Americans stayed back to help while others fanned out to explore the village. Several of us took a walk along the beach and went for a swim where we befriended a couple of ten-year-olds who were learning to float.

As another woman and I steadied the boys by holding our hands under their backsides, I said to my companion, "When I move out here, I think this little guy will be my friend."

Meanwhile a couple of American teenagers joined some Haitian children in a pick-up soccer match while others cheered from the sidelines. On the way back from the beach, I talked with some of the villagers and held a little baby whose mother was tending a bubbling pot of beans. Everyone seemed curious and they didn't seem to mind having company.

"What's going on? Who are all these *blancs*? Why are the men building benches?" several people asked me.

"The Christian mission in St. Louis du Nord has just bought some property over there," I replied, pointing toward the road we had come in on. "This evening we're going to dedicate the land to God."

"What are you going to do with it?" someone piped up.

"The mission plans to open a medical clinic," I said, again feeling a spark of excitement. "And we're also hoping to start a school in a year or so, God willing."

"That sounds like a good idea," one tall man in his twenties said approvingly.

"Yes, we need a clinic and school for our children," added a young woman, perhaps his wife.

I invited them to come to the dedication service that night and bring their family and friends.

That evening as the sun began to drop behind the hills, we all gathered on the land where the hastily built benches awaited us. Local residents crowded onto the benches with us as Janeil faced the crowd against the backdrop of the painted sky. Attracted by the lights and music, many more curious villagers arrived and stood around the edges.

"Lord, we're gathered here this evening to dedicate this land for the advancement of your Kingdom. We ask your presence and guidance that what we are doing is according to your will. Thank you that some local people have joined us this evening and are interested in what we are doing. Help us to be good neighbors and to serve you faithfully. We pray that they will understand our purpose and will spread the word among their friends."

Accompanied by a loud electric guitar, we sang "Lord, I Lift Your Name on High," first in English and then in Creole.

> "*Segnè mwen beni non ou…*
> *nan tonbo monte nan syel*
> *Segnè mwen beni non ou.*"

The enthusiastic singing wavered when several of the flimsy benches began to collapse sideways in slow motion. Obviously, the weight and movement of so many people was more than they could handle. However people just picked themselves up and continued to sing.

Janeil read several passages of Scripture and held out his right hand toward the land and the surrounding hills. I was reminded of Joel 2:28-29.

> "Your sons and daughters will prophesy, your old
> men will dream dreams, your young men will see
> visions. Even on my servants, both men and
> women, I will pour out my Spirit in those days."

Yes, I thought, Janeil is truly a young man with a vision. I'd like to be a part of his dream and help get this new satellite mission started.

Before we settled down to sleep that night on the newly dedicated land, I pulled Janeil aside.

"You know, Janeil, living out here would feel like the clinic in Marchand Dessalines where I served twenty years ago. That kind of frontier medicine really appeals to me. I'm thinking that the main mission is running smoothly and the feeding programs are well established. I'd really like to move out here permanently."

"I can't say I'm surprised," he said with a smile. "In fact, I kind of thought of you when we bought this land. It won't be easy to fill your shoes in St. Louis, but if this is where your heart is, I'd certainly support you."

That night as I lay under the endless stars, I thanked God for this new challenge and opportunity. I hadn't dreamed when Lisa and I were talking the previous morning that, at age seventy-three, I'd find myself beginning another new adventure. I couldn't have been more excited.

CHAPTER TWENTY-THREE

About four months after the dedication, five people came in from Cincinnati to help lay the foundation at the Baie. The money for the materials to construct the building had come from a grant through the Cincinnati Presbytery. I spent the week helping lay concrete forms for the large structure that would include my new home. We experienced a couple of unusual incidents during that week.

One day we had put out the word that we'd pay for five lobsters for our evening meal, but we hadn't yet developed any relationships in the area. This wasn't an extravagance, for lobster was not uncommon in the bay's waters. A group of men came by and offered to trap and prepare their catch for our dinner. However, when they returned, they'd brought a sea crab and only four lobsters. They wanted extra for the crab, but I refused since they'd promised five lobsters, not four. Although they argued for quite awhile, they finally agreed to the original terms, and our dinner that night was excellent. It turned out that the leader had formerly been a chef at a hotel.

I subsequently learned that they were actually a gang of thieves! The leader had been fired from his chef's job because he'd been caught stealing. He even "lifted" a knife from one of us, but our Haitian interpreter followed him and got it back.

We found out later that they'd been arrested and imprisoned in Port-au-Prince.

The second occurrence happened the night before we were to leave. A group of guys we didn't know was hanging around the concrete slab in front of the "disco" where we had pitched our tents. We had heard a rumor that they were going to rob us, and the other two women in the group stayed awake most of the night, too nervous to sleep.

"Miss Pat, how can you be so trusting and sleep so well?" they asked the next morning, for I had enjoyed my usual good night's rest.

"I guess I've just learned to 'let go and let God,'" I said with a chuckle and a shrug.

We laid the foundation in November of 2003. Plans called for a large concrete block building that would include my living quarters, a spacious general-purpose room, the clinic, and storage areas, all topped by a high flat concrete roof. It would also have a long porch clear across the front. Although there would be no running water or electricity at first and I would have only an outhouse, I was eager to begin my life there. Construction progressed enough over the next few months that I could move to the Baie in June of 2004.

I lived very primitively for a year or so, taking sponge baths out of buckets and using water that a local man lugged from the nearby community spigot for laundry and dishes. There were several of these spigots throughout the village where people could go to fill their plastic containers for about fifteen Haitian dollars a year. A different mission had brought clean water to the community years earlier by piping it in from the surrounding mountains. It was fine to drink "as is," but when groups came in, we did take the precaution of treating it with a few drops of Clorox.

Anamarie, whom I had come to know well over the years as she cooked for the nutrition programs, moved out to the Baie to be my housekeeper. I rented a room for her in a house that had a tin roof and a cement floor, a definite improvement over the dirt floor of her home in St. Louis.

I started the clinic as soon as I got settled at the Baie. In no time at all, I was very busy. One of my first cases was something I'd heard about but never seen.

"Èske ou ka ede pitit fi m?"

A young mother handed her little girl to me asking for help in a soft calm voice. As I unwrapped a dirty strip of cloth from the child's foot, I saw that the flesh on two of her toes was mangled.

"What happened?" I asked in Creole.

"A rat bit my baby. I heard her cry out last night and got to her just as it was disappearing through a hole in the wall. Can you help her?" she asked again.

I cleaned the wounds thoroughly with hydrogen peroxide, put in a couple of stitches to close the deeper one, applied some antibiotic ointment, and bandaged the foot.

"Bring her back in two days so I can change the dressing," I said. As I gave the girl back to her mother, I put my hands on both their shoulders and prayed for God's healing touch.

Such emergencies cropped up nearly every day. People would gather very early outside the blue metal door leading to the small exam room and tiny windowed "pharmacy." Each day I gave out twenty cards, which meant that I was actually seeing forty to sixty people daily, for patients inevitably brought along other family members who were sick. I was grateful for the way God had equipped me for this ministry through five years in Rosemary's clinic two decades earlier.

One day while people were lined up waiting to see me, two men carried in an unconscious man who had been in a moped accident. He was badly hurt, and I did the best I could to treat his injuries. As soon as I stabilized him, another man who had been seriously cut using a machete was helped in. Once again the people outside had to wait as I treated and sewed up his wound. Just as I finally called the next person in line, yet another emergency came in. This man had fallen down the mountain and had a broken arm that needed to be set.

"Lord, give me strength," I prayed. "I can't keep up with the regular patients and treat all these emergencies too. Help me find a way to cope." Then I took a deep breath and got back to work.

It was almost sunset before I finished seeing patients that afternoon. I felt totally drained. From that day on, I lightened my workload by giving out only fifteen cards.

Hunger was also a serious problem at the Baie, just as had been the case wherever I served in Haiti. Before long, we managed to start a limited feeding program for the elderly based on the one at the St. Louis compound.

Anamarie's help was invaluable in making things run smoothly. No matter how busy we were, I could always count on her to maintain a calm cheerful attitude with a friendly smile. Besides keeping house for me, she did the marketing and washed my clothes. About once a week she went out to the front porch with two five-gallon buckets and a long stick of lye soap. She hung my clean dresses on the clothesline outside the house and later pressed them with a heavy iron. It was made of cast iron and had a hinged cover where she added charcoal to heat it. She also helped me immensely by cooking for the mission groups who visited us. I frequently heard her singing as she worked. I was the only white woman at the Baie, and Anamarie became like a daughter to me.

When I first settled at the satellite campus, I knew that I would also need a trustworthy Haitian man to work for me. I asked around in St. Louis if anyone knew of someone who might be willing to move out there.

"You should talk with Michel," Jude suggested. "He's a really good worker, and I'm sure you could count on him."

I didn't know Michel very well, but I decided to take Jude's recommendation and see if he'd be interested.

"I need to discuss it with Jenise," he said. "The Baie would be a long way from our families here in St Louis."

The next morning he reported that they'd like to take me up on my offer.

"I'm so glad," I said, shaking his hand. "But I do have one request. If you're going to come with me, I'd like for you and Jenise to get married."

A disappointed look crossed his face.

"The only reason we aren't is because we can't afford a wedding."

I had heard that excuse many times before.

"If that's all that's standing in your way, I'll help you pay for it," I said. "I really believe that parents should be married."

We decided that Michel would move in June when I did, he and Jenise would marry in August, and then the rest of their family would join him. I never regretted the decision to hire him, for he proved to be a very trustworthy worker and a loyal friend.

It took almost two years before we finally got solar panels and therefore electricity. Until then I had no lights in the evening, and we could only use hand or battery-operated tools and appliances. Eventually we got a small generator and could power the tools and lights if we needed them beyond the solar power. We could even use an electric hand mixer when cooking for groups.

What a treat to be able to relax with a good book after dark! I loved reading my Louis L'Amour paperbacks to unwind before bed.

That spring I decided to plant a garden. Things grew well in the soil next to my house once we rigged up a simple irrigation system. I hoped people would see by this example how they might supplement their own food supply. However, until we put up a fence, goats and pigs got more of the vegetables than we did!

A strong pot of coffee had long been a source of pleasure for me, and at the Baie, making homemade bread also became a simple joy. Before that if we wanted bread, we had to send to Padepe to buy it for five Haitian dollars a loaf, plus another ten dollars for the tap-tap. So I decided to learn to bake bread from "scratch." We bought flour by the hundred-pound bag, and I baked every two days using our propane gas oven. I liked kneading the dough and smelling the fresh golden loaves. When groups came in, I would bake twice a day for breakfast and supper. The Haitian workers from St. Louis always looked forward to my bread with peanut butter and bananas for breakfast.

"Miss Pat, where did you get your recipe for this wonderful bread?" asked a woman from Indiana one day. "I gave up trying to bake bread because mine never came out as light as yours."

People always wanted to know my secret. "It's nothing special," I answered honestly. "I just got it out of a cookbook." But they found that hard to believe.

I did get a nasty surprise one morning when a pair of beady little eyes looked up at me as I reached into the bag of flour. Startled, I saw that there was an entire family of mice living in the pantry. Anamarie had noticed signs of them in the kitchen, but this was the first time I'd actually seen them. No doubt about it, they had to go!

After trying unsuccessfully to get rid of the critters with poison, I asked a Haitian friend if he knew anyone who had kittens. The first two I acquired took care of the problem, but they soon disappeared. That wasn't all bad because one of them was always underfoot, sometimes causing me to stumble. I certainly didn't need to fall and break a bone! Finally, I got a third kitten, and we gave her the unique name of Cat. She was a good mouser and managed to survive, even though Haitians sometimes eat cat on special occasions. In fact, several offered me replacement kittens if I would give Cat away to be eaten for someone's birthday dinner!

Another important part of my routine was to prepare the communion elements every Sunday for the small congregation of ten or so who attended church at the Baie. Since people had to bring chairs to sit on, I arranged to donate a few benches to serve as pews. A lay pastor had founded the church several years before I moved out there. He took his responsibility very seriously even though he didn't have any formal training for the ministry. From time to time he would invite Janeil to preach. When a short-term group was there on a Sunday, they really swelled the numbers and were a source of encouragement to their Haitian brothers and sisters in Christ.

"Miss Pat, are you happy that you moved out to the Baie?" Americans would frequently ask. "It's beautiful, but it's so isolated. Seems like it would be really hard with no other *blancs* for company."

My answer was always the same.

"I do sometimes miss 'woman talk' or being with other people my age, but I love it out here and have made some wonderful friends. I'm happy to be serving here, and I enjoy my quiet time in the evenings. God knew that this was the best place for me at this point in my life."

CHAPTER TWENTY-FOUR

After two major floods in three years during which three to six feet of muddy water poured through my house, it became clear that we had built in a flood plain. I thought we should have figured that out before building, but no one in the community could remember anything like these severe floods. I was grateful that local men came to my aid each time I was flooded out.

I recall that soon after the second flood, several young Haitians appeared at my door to help shovel out the mud and wash down the walls.

After we'd been mopping for what seemed like forever, I paused and asked, "Would you fellows like to stop for a breather?"

I listened while they rested their backs and talked about the recent flood.

"My wife had to stand up all night holding our baby to keep her off the muddy floor," one said. "She's a good woman."

I'd often heard such stories about the hardships Haitian women face any time it rains.

"These last two floods are the worst I've seen in my whole life," another fellow added. "The creek nearly washed my neighbor's house away!"

I have to admit, one good thing that came out of the floods was my bonding with these good-hearted folks.

Although I had a bedroom on the ground floor, my room was very hot, and my favorite place to spend the night was in a sleeping bag on the roof. Mosquitoes weren't a problem at the Baie, and there was always a breeze up there. During the first year I had to climb a twenty-foot wooden ladder to reach the roof. I was grateful when an American group poured a long flight of concrete stairs, which made the roof more easily accessible. After that, groups could pitch their tents or sleep on mattresses in the open air. I never tired of admiring God's handiwork as I lay under the star-filled sky.

That staircase did lead to one very upsetting experience, however. One night when it was raining hard, I went to bed in my room downstairs. A few hours later, I woke up because of the heat and realized that the rain had stopped. I decided to go up to the roof for the rest of the night.

Just a week earlier, some solar panels had been stolen from a house nearby. As I climbed the stairs that night, I realized that Michel was asleep at the top of the steps, guarding our newly installed panels. Since I knew that he slept very soundly, I thought I could slip by without awakening him. But as I moved past him, he jumped up, thinking I was a thief.

"What are you doing up here?" he shouted as he shoved me all the way down to the concrete floor below.

I hit my head and was knocked out cold. When I came to, I saw Michel's anxious face above me.

"Miss Pat, Miss Pat, wake up! Are you okay? I'm so sorry. I thought somebody was robbing us!"

"I'm not sure," I said groggily, "but can you help me get back upstairs where it's cooler?"

Although my ankle was killing me, I was able to scoot back up the stairs where Michel gave me his bed to lie on. He felt so guilty that he didn't sleep a wink the rest of the night.

Somehow I did manage to get some rest, and the next morning I was surprised to see that the pillow was covered with blood. Until then I hadn't realized that I'd cut my head. Since my right ankle and foot were swollen nearly twice their normal size, I was pretty sure I had broken something. How was I going to get back downstairs, and who would stitch up my head? I looked around for Michel, but he was nowhere to be found. Evidently I was on my own. I crawled over to the top step and with my one good leg, slowly eased my way downstairs on my bottom.

"Jenise! Michel!" I called. "Where are you? I need you!"

Jenise came running in from the kitchen. Her eyes were red from crying.

"Oh, Miss Pat, your head is bleeding."

Her hands were trembling as she reached toward me, and when she found the gash, I heard her gasp.

"I wish Anamarie were here. She'd know what to do."

"Let's stay calm, Jenise. Since Anamarie is at market getting supplies for our lunch guests, we'll just have to make do for a while. It's a good thing that Dr. Fadou and the American medical team are stopping here today on their way to Beauchamp," I said, picturing the Haitian government doctor who worked at the mission in St. Louis. "He'll be able to check me over."

"Is there anything I can do for you right now, Miss Pat?"

"Yes, please go get a cloth and some water so you can wash my cut. We'll also need some gauze from the clinic. And after that, I'll want my usual cup of coffee," I added, attempting to lighten the mood.

"Michel feels very bad about what he did to you," Jenise said, her voice quivering with emotion as she washed my head. "You know how much he loves you. He'd never want to hurt you!"

"I know," I said reassuringly.

I think Jenise felt better once she was able to help me. She brought in a rocking chair from the front porch and a box to prop up my foot. Just the smell of the steaming coffee made me feel better.

But as the morning progressed, everything began to hurt. My whole body was black and blue, and my head and my ankle and foot were throbbing. Anamarie got back and found some Tylenol that helped a little, but sometimes I still had to grit my teeth. Would the group from the mission ever get here? I wondered.

"Dear Lord, I don't mind a little pain, but I'm really hurting. Can you please get the mission group here soon?"

Finally, I heard the sound of the truck pulling up out front. What a relief that a doctor would soon be able to examine me.

"Dr. Fadou! Dr. Fadou!" I heard Michel calling frantically as the driver cut the engine. "Come fast. I hurt Miss Pat!"

I hadn't seen Michel all morning. It was as if he'd been avoiding me. Soon he and the doctor appeared in the doorway.

"Am I ever glad to see you," I said with relief.

"Can't say that I expected to have you for a patient, Miss Pat," the doctor said, pulling some gloves from his medical bag. "It looks as if you need several stitches on the back of your head, and then we'll check out that ankle."

I had no intention of revealing the details of my accident, but suddenly a torrent of Creole came pouring out of Michel's mouth as he confessed his role in the mishap to the interpreters with the group. "It's all my fault, but I didn't mean to hurt her!"

I winced as the doctor put seven stitches in my head before he turned his attention to my now purplish foot.

In the meantime the dozen or so folks who had come for the mobile medical clinic in Beauchamp had gathered around my new fourteen-foot table. Jeremy, a one-year missionary in St. Louis, had just finished making it for me a few weeks earlier. He had pre-cut the wood and transported it to the Baie where he assembled and stained the table in the large common room. The medical team was talking quietly across the smooth planks of the tabletop while the doctor tended my injuries.

As the doctor finished wrapping my ankle in an ace bandage, a nurse named Melinda came over to confer with Dr. Fadou.

"I'd really like to get an x-ray of that foot, Miss Pat, but we're scheduled to be in Beauchamp for the next couple of days," the doctor said as Melinda looked on.

"Do you think you can stand to wait until next week when this group leaves for the States?" she asked. "Or do we need to find a way to send you sooner?"

"Give me a couple of days to see how I feel. Either way, I'm afraid I'm not going to be good for much," I said ruefully.

That afternoon I traveled in the cab of the truck to Beauchamp, the newest mission location about four miles away. All I could do was sit and watch everyone else work as they organized their supplies for the next morning's clinic. How I hated being laid up when there was so much to do, but I simply couldn't put any weight on that ankle.

"Dear God, I don't like ask for special favors. So please help me 'tough it out' until next week when these folks go home."

Every couple of hours for the rest of the day, Melinda checked in to see if I needed anything.

"Here's some Tylenol and a cup of coffee, Miss Pat," she said with a smile, sitting down to take a break. "Rumor has it you love your coffee."

"Thanks so much, Melinda," I said, taking a sip. "You know, I'm feeling a little aggravated about this ankle. I broke the very same one five or six years ago on the way up the mountain to the church in La Croix."

"Twice on the same ankle! How did that happen?" she asked, leaning in to hear the rest of the story.

"A girl in our group was taken sick and started vomiting. As I started down the mountainside looking for some shade where she could rest, I stepped into a hole and snapped my ankle. It hurt like the dickens."

"How did they ever get you back to the mission?"

"Fortunately, one of the Americans had been a military corpsman. He made a kind of splint from a piece of plastic he found, you know the kind mechanics use to lie on under a car."

"That was really resourceful," Melinda said admiringly.

"Not only that, the men took off their ties to secure the plastic around my ankle. Sorry to say, none of us made it to church that morning. It took them two hours to get the sick girl and me down the mountain to our pickup truck.

"Thankfully my ankle healed up fine that time," I said, grimacing as I shifted in my chair. "It just goes to show that it's hard to keep this 'old girl' down!"

The week passed fairly quickly. Someone had left a Louis L'Amour novel behind, and before long, I was totally immersed in the "Wild West." I also took a lot of naps, both in Beauchamp and back at the mission. When I finally saw my doctor in Illinois, the breaks in my ankle and foot had already started to mend. All he did was put me in a walking cast and let the bones finish healing naturally.

CHAPTER TWENTY-FIVE

Janeil became Executive Director of the mission in 2007, ushering in a whole new generation of missionaries who stepped up in response to God's call to serve in Haiti. I began to think about retiring, but I didn't want to quit before someone was in place to oversee the programs at the Baie. During my final year there, a young married couple spent several months with me, learning and observing, and finding the focus that would define the direction their ministry would take.

Their style was different from mine, but our goals were the same—to bring the love of Jesus in practical concrete ways to people who needed it. Whereas my service had its roots in "country doctoring," my replacements longed to help people become more self-sufficient. Their emphasis was on agriculture, and they hoped to empower the community by showing and teaching people how to get better yields from their subsistence gardens.

"Do you have any advice for us, Miss Pat, on how to relate to the people out here? We'd like to tap into your wisdom," the husband said, acknowledging my experience.

"You know, people are people, wherever they are and whatever their circumstances, but we don't have to talk them to death. I've found that if you're trying to earn someone's trust, it's best to listen a lot and only offer an opinion when you're asked for one. How we treat people is more evangelistic than words."

"I guess that means we need to trust God to guide us in nurturing new relationships," the wife responded. "I know that he has called us here, and we have so many hopes and plans for our ministry."

"God will work through you just as he has through me, but it will take time and patience on your part. Most important, though, we missionaries have to remember that *our* work can't make any lasting difference. Jesus already did the hard work. Whatever we do is our response, and the results are God's."

After I retired, I thought I'd be done with broken bones, but that wasn't to be the case. When I returned home from Haiti, I went to live with Susan and Jerry. By now he had become a pastor with his wife's blessing. One day I went for a bike ride and took a tumble. At the time it didn't seem very serious. However, a couple of weeks later, my right hip gave out on me, and I fell in the house. The pain was excruciating, and I realized that I must have broken my hip.

"Susan, I can't stand this pain. I think you'll have to take me to the hospital," I said through clenched teeth.

"I haven't seen you cry very often, Mom, so it must really hurt. You just lie still," she said, snatching a throw pillow for me from the sofa. "I'll phone Jerry at the church, and we'll take you to the hospital. Or would you rather I call an ambulance?"

"No, you and Jerry can help me to the garage and into the back seat. I don't want to have to pay for an ambulance," I said, but I winced at the thought of trying to get into the car.

We managed somehow to make it to the hospital where I was helped onto a gurney and admitted. We assumed that

I would see an orthopedic surgeon and be operated on that afternoon.

"We're sorry, but there's no orthopedist on duty over the weekend," the ER doctor said. "We'll try to keep you as comfortable as possible with pain medicine."

"I don't tolerate pain medications very well," I said to the nurse. "They make me delirious. I'd rather try to 'tough it out' until Monday."

I don't know when I have prayed as hard as I did that weekend. I asked God to help me deal with the pain. I also prayed that some good would come from my ordeal, but I couldn't imagine what that would be.

Finally the orthopedic surgeon arrived early on Monday morning and he did a hip replacement on me. When the anesthetic wore off, the same nurse who had been on duty Friday was standing by my bed.

"Pat, you are one strong lady. I don't know how you made it through the weekend. I want you to know that from now on, no one else will have to endure what you did. The hospital board has determined that we will always have an orthopedist on call. Such a policy should have been in place a long time ago."

As the nurse left the room, I said a quick prayer.

"Thank you, Lord, for your support during these past three days. I praise you for using me to make life easier for someone else."

Before I drifted off to sleep, I recalled Romans 8:28. "…all things work together for good to those who love God. "

What a privilege, even from a hospital bed in Illinois, to still be used for his glory.

A few months after my surgery, I returned to Haiti for a final farewell. Leaving the people I had served and loved was one of the hardest things I've ever had to do. But remembering all the many hugs and expressions of gratitude as I left gives me a sense of warmth each time I think back on my service there.

"*Bondye beni ou, Mis Pat,*" Anamarie said, embracing me as I walked to the mission truck on my last morning at the Baie. "I'll never forget you. I love you like my own mother."

I'd said good-bye the night before to Michel and Jenise, and they didn't come around again. I was relieved since leaving Anamarie was difficult enough. I couldn't have handled separating from them too on that heart-wrenching day.

As Janeil drove the mission truck away from my home of four years, I looked out the back window where I saw a circle of my Haitian friends waving in the distance. I couldn't hold back the tears any longer.

Janeil glanced over at me as he turned onto the main road.

"Are you okay, Miss Pat?" he asked me gently.

"I will be," I responded. "Just give me a few minutes."

I folded my hands in my lap, bowed my head, and silently thanked the Lord for inspiring me to spend twenty-five years here in Haiti.

"I praise you, God, for giving me a heart to serve your people and for using me to make a difference in their lives. My life has been made richer by sharing their faith and friendship and courage. Thank you, Lord."

I felt a peace after that prayer and looked up to give Janeil a smile as we made our way through the arid land past the sprawling cacti, donkey trains, and people waving and shouting *bonswa* to us as we neared the Big River.

EPILOGUE

Pat Hamilton has been a true inspiration to hundreds of people whose lives she has touched, both Haitian and American. Her impact on the mission continues to be felt, for numerous programs that she initiated are thriving to this day. Many of the people with whom she crossed paths are still serving and praising God, wherever they are!

The authors had the privilege of attending her retirement party in Ramsey, Illinois, in 2008, where a variety of people spoke in praise of her selflessness in particular.

The mission team from her son-in-law's church said that knowing her had changed their outlook on life. "She's the most loving Christian I've ever been around," one member said.

A board member of the Northwest Haiti Christian Mission drove 150 miles after church that day to honor her because of the thousands of souls she's reached as a faithful servant of the Lord Jesus Christ.

"Miss Pat's life is a wonderful example of Christian service and evangelism," he said sincerely. "I once heard her say, 'I really think our actions and how we treat people are more evangelistic than words.' She'll never know how much I love and respect her."

Magdala, the nurse midwife mentioned in the book, wrote to share her immense love and respect for her friend of twenty years.

"Known as *Mis Pat* by most Haitians, this nickname is the expression of the affection and trust of those people who can't afford to pay for food or buy medicine for themselves and their families.

"We all considered her as a mother in the mission. She was always smiling. She always had good advice to give. At the beginning she was the only nurse in the clinic. She had to hold the consultations and give the patients the medicines they needed. It's with the same heart that she used to feed the deprived children at the nutritional program. She couldn't bear to see children suffering, so she always tried to supply their needs.

"For me personally she was like a mother. I came to her in 1994 when I was pregnant, whenever I had a question about marriage, pregnancy, or any other subject. She never showed any signs of impatience when I came to her.

"I think she was and will remain a mother for anyone who worked or is still working at the mission. There is so much more I could say about Miss Pat. I am convinced that only Heaven can reward her for what she did in Haiti, especially in Saint Louis du Nord."

Miss Pat's "adopted" son Navius also had many appreciative comments to contribute. Now in his twenties, he recalled, "The first day she and I met, we 'clicked' and were together from then on. Growing up without my real parents didn't bother me at all because Miss Pat loved me like I came from her womb. She's the reason why I'm still here today.

"I saw her work at the mission as impeccable. She had a heart for her work. She's like an Energizer battery. Whenever anyone needed something or had a cut, she would stop what she was doing to help that person. All I can say to her is, 'Well done'!"

Navius likes to write poetry, and Miss Pat was his inspiration for the following stanza.

When You Smile
When you smile, it is like
the beginning of a new day.
It shakes the dust from
yesterday's problems
and makes today joyful
and tranquil.

Maureen Moore, the Lab and Pharmacy Director at the mission, shared the following tribute about her good friend and fellow missionary.

"I have thought long and hard about what to say about Miss Pat, and there just aren't words to express how I feel.

"She was there all those times that I was overwhelmed with how I could help and who I should help and how was the best way to do it. Her gentle quiet spirit really helped me through all those times when I wasn't sure I could continue.

"She is a beautiful Christian woman. If she hadn't been here when I came to Northwest Haiti Christian Mission, I probably wouldn't still be serving here today.

"I have many cherished memories of our times together, and I miss her more than I can say. I wish her much joy in her retirement. I love her very much."

The final tribute to Miss Pat came from Janeil Owen, the Executive Director of the Northwest Haiti Christian Mission.

"As a second-generation missionary, I have been on and around the mission field all of my life. The mission field as a vocation is a pretty difficult life. To be called to the poorest zone of the poorest country in the Western Hemisphere is on another level entirely. In the past thirty-plus years, I have seen a lot of people come into the northwest zone of Haiti and be broken by it. I have seen others who have thrived in the work God has called them to.

"There has never been anyone greater than Miss Pat. Known throughout the zone for her love, dedication and her ability to connect with the people of Haiti, she was never short of inspiration or the ability to motivate others to achieve their best.

"My dad always said of Miss Pat, 'If she was a bird and you tried to cook her, you would have to cook her for hours and hours...' Miss Pat is a tough old bird that has been through much. She is steadfast in her dedication to her Heavenly Father and those in Haiti that she loved and served.

"Miss Pat had a profound impact on my life, helping to shape me into the man I am today. She encouraged me in her faithfulness to explore all the new doors that God presented. She was and is a quietly courageous woman who invested her life in others."

In her typical humble manner, when asked for her own input about her retirement, Pat responded, "I'm just grateful God used me for those exciting things. Isn't He a great God?"

Would you like to see your manuscript become a book?

If you are interested in becoming a PublishAmerica author, please submit your manuscript for possible publication to us at:

acquisitions@publishamerica.com

You may also mail in your manuscript to:

**PublishAmerica
PO Box 151
Frederick, MD 21705**

We also offer free graphics for Children's Picture Books!

---

www.publishamerica.com

CPSIA information can be obtained at www.ICGtesting.com
Printed in the USA
BVOW040129200613

323789BV00002B/27/P